Stranger
by the River

Zoomie
I hope you will
find words of truth
and comfort in this
book. Love Lady

Available from ECKANKAR:

Ask the Master, Book 1
Earth to God, Come In Please . . .
ECKANKAR—Ancient Wisdom for Today
The Wind of Change
Soul Travelers of the Far Country
Child in the Wilderness
The Spiritual Exercises of ECK

The Mahanta Transcripts Series

Journey of Soul, Book 1
How to Find God, Book 2
The Secret Teachings, Book 3
The Golden Heart, Book 4
Cloak of Consciousness, Book 5
Unlocking the Puzzle Box, Book 6
The Eternal Dreamer, Book 7
The Dream Master, Book 8

Also available from ECKANKAR:

ECKANKAR—The Key to Secret Worlds
The Shariyat-Ki-Sugmad, Books One and Two
The Spiritual Notebook
The Tiger's Fang

Authorized ECKANKAR edition.

Stranger by the River

Paul Twitchell

ECKANKAR
Minneapolis, MN

Stranger by the River

Printed in U.S.A.

Cover design by Lois Stanfield
Illustrations by Signy Cohen

Third Edition—1987
Third Printing—1994

Publisher's Cataloging in Publication
(Prepared by Quality Books Inc.)

Twitchell, Paul, 1908–1971.
    Stranger by the river / Paul Twitchell.—3rd ed., authorized
ECKANKAR ed.
    p. cm.
    Preassigned LCCN: 88-80197.
    ISBN 1-57043-038-1

    1. Spiritual life. 2. Eckankar. 3. Twitchell, Paul, 1908–1971.
I. Title.

BP605.E3T89 1994   299'.93
                                    QBI93-21810

Dedicated to
GAIL
for her love and
patience

Contents

The River

here was the river.

There was always the river. No matter how many seasons had arched over the rim of time, the river was there, still flowing onward silently and quietly to the sea.

It passed down from the mighty Himalayas where the earth was filled with the dust of those who walked the land.

The water was like the river of God. It was always flowing outward and onward, always a symbol, always going onward to join with the waters of other rivers, and moving onward to the waters of the shining ocean.

The seeker had reached the side of this great river and stopped here to stay. He no longer drifted with the tide of mankind which moved through the world like logs at the mercy of the storm on the river's surface.

He observed the river again. This was a beautiful land marked by rivers and creeks. The river is joined by the clear water of another before the levee of Srinagar. Separating them for considerable distance is the island which hides a part of the far shore.

He sat on the bank under the sleepy willows, watching the sluggish eddies pass, wondering at his life. He had returned home again, like the prodigal son, but his father was not here to greet him. Sorrow filled him.

Then he looked up and saw the majestic figure clothed in a maroon robe standing nearby. There was a smile on his lips, and great compassion in those coal black eyes. The swarthy face was half-hidden by a short, black beard.

A joy leaped in the seeker's heart.

His search was over. Rebazar Tarzs, the Sat Guru was there to welcome him home.

The Seeker

H e was the seeker.

He was like any other man, and it could have been you.

Outwardly, his life was little different from that of other people—working, toiling, laboring—yet his struggle to find life was deeper and more acute; the pain was greater, the suffering unbearable, and his sensitivity more intense.

Nothing could lift him spiritually, and the responsibility or success which other men had would not touch him. He was the outcast, the lonely, and the dejected, for love had passed him by as there was nothing in his life which love had to anchor upon.

Yet he was always the seeker. The seeker of something that lay continually beyond his reach. Eagerly he sought that mystical something in the heart of a rose, the face of a child, or the tenderness of a woman. He could not find the love that his life was spent in seeking.

His search had carried him across the world and back again to the river, where he sat on the bank wondering if the answer would ever be found, until that day when the Tibetan in the maroon robe came and sat beside him.

Then he saw the light that came from beyond, that grew in an ever-greater, ever-widening circle. And he saw the woman, the slender, long-limbed woman with dark eyes, who stood at the edge of the light.

He knew that whatever it was, deep within him were worlds invisible, and all that he sought was love. That the form was only the instrument through which love seeks its way into the world.

Rebazar Tarzs rubbed his strong chin and said, "Thou art the seeker, but there are others too, countless millions, walking before thee, behind thee, or beside thee. The answer is God—and God lies within as Jesus said that day upon the mountainside, 'The kingdom of God is within you!'"

The seeker looked at the slow, muddy waters of the river flowing through the heart of the land, and wondered.

All the world became light and a strange humming sound entered into his heart, giving him peace. All wisdom, understanding, love, and knowledge was revealed to him in the gently murmuring water, ever moving toward the sea.

"Ah, the river," he said softly to the Tibetan. "It is like life! I beg thee, Master, give me the wisdom and glory of God!"

The Tibetan opened his mouth and began to speak.

The Light of God

ake thy position as I, by sitting with both feet crossed beneath thee and gaze gently and sweetly into the Spiritual Eye between the eyebrows."

So the seeker looked into the space between the brows minutely and more minutely. Everything was dark. Then came the Light, a blinding sheet of white Light.

The Light came from within him, a great sun throwing its glittering, brilliant rays in a circle around him. Its brilliancy was greater than ten thousand suns.

The Light became greater until it hurt his Spiritual Eye to gaze into It. He was conscious of squinting, as though his eyes were looking into the center of the Light.

Then he realized the Light was from within himself. It spread into an ever-widening circle until It filled the whole universe, flowing out of a center within himself. It became a burning beacon, until his whole body pulsed with the rhythm of Its surging waves like the pounding of surf upon a sandy beach.

A roaring in his ears became louder until he could hardly stand the Sound, and then into his inner vision stepped the Master in his maroon robe, walking toward him. He recognized the radiant form of the Guru.

The vision began to speak. "I am the Light. The Light which shines within thee. The Light that fills the world. From me spring all things, all beings, and all universes.

"I am that Sound. That Word within thee. That Sound fills all the worlds and sustains all universes.

"There is no time, no space within my cosmic body. I am the living God; the knowledge you seek, the wisdom and understanding and love.

"I am eternal for there never was a time when I did not exist, nor was there ever anything in all of space which I have not been, and am not now a part of.

"The infinite universes are my body, the ethers my blood, the worlds my bones, and the suns my heart. When you came out of me, like a child out of the womb, you came to express love, as did my messengers Jesus, Yaubl Sacabi, Krishna, Rama, Milarepa, and Buddha, for love is my life. Without love neither thee nor I can exist. Without love there would be absolutely nothing. Can you imagine an absolute void which would be all space without life?

"My love supports the universes and worlds. It gives thee the seasons for the harvests. My love unites all things; the minerals and earth are one, as are the flowers and the grass, the bee and its honey. One cannot live without the other. I am in all things and all things are within me.

"Man is united with woman by my cords of love, and the child to the mother, and the circle is complete for all things are bound together in love. But then again, all life is united with me by love, for it is only by my love that life does exist upon this planet and in all worlds, universes, and space.

"Love is all. There is nothing more. I am love and love is myself. Love is life and life is love. Love me and live, but hate and die for there is no greater death than by hate.

"You must desire me, love me, more than you do all other things; love me above your own Soul.

"Love is the only thing I can give thee, and all I have to give thee. From out of my body springs all life, because I love all life. To love me is to be free, for he who loves me will see me, and to him will be given all the wisdom which is mine.

"I am he whom you know as the Lord. I am the Light of the Soul, the Music of the spheres. I Am that I Am, and the Light of the worlds! I am God, the living love of eternity!"

The seeker opened his eyes and looked around at

the beautiful waters moving slowly past the green willows. His eyes came to rest upon the Tibetan's face.

Rebazar Tarzs asked, "What did you see?"

"Thee," replied the seeker.

The Tibetan nodded, smiling.

The Call of Soul

he willows dipped their green leafy hands into the waters. Spider webs were white patches of wet tent tops over the long slender branches; and the river, always the river kept flowing past at his feet.

He gazed at it thinking that this was the great river, with its life and sounds of whistles and slushing wheels, that expressed a state of feeling within himself. Rebazar Tarzs placed a brown finger in the muddy waters, then looked at the seeker.

He said, "Can you think of life to be no more than what it is at this moment? When the pattern of love and joy rushes into your world to find it empty?

"I have been with thee through the centuries. There have been moments when you have found life so empty. You have awakened in the deep night, to find the rain softly singing through the gutters of the roof and the wind whispering in the trees, but thy mind on God, yet a lonely God.

"You always knew that somewhere in this world was the Sat Guru for you. Maybe a beggar, a monk, a rich or dying man, or a woman whose words would seize thee with a love that would make thee give up everything to follow the call through fire or stone walls, over mountains or plains or seas to me, the Master.

"Was it thy thoughts or imagination that made thee always hear the beautiful melody? Some said that it was the call of Soul, and at those times you were ready to give up and make the sacrifice.

"Until now you had not found the person upon whose words you could hang breathlessly, or who gave thee that feeling of such joy you felt thy next breath would be the last, and hoped that thou wouldst die with an experience of sheer bliss.

"Then you came to me, and I will tell thee this. I am thy self. My call is the thin, biting wind that blows from the mountain heights. I am the agony of thy heart when thy beloved has turned from thee, and you struggle to regain that precious moment again. I am the cry of the child in the lonely night for its mother, and the loneliness of the aged.

"My call is that desire to find God. But once you find your true mate, the counterpart of myself, Holy Self, the desire is fulfilled, for then you have started on the journey to God's heights.

"Thou art fulfilling the great expectation of every Soul that manifests in a body on earth, and that is through love. For love is the only and noblest force in all the universes. By doing this you become the clay in my hands, and this is known as surrender, for I take the affairs of thy being into my hands on every plane, and this is in reality, my hands.

"First, thou must be seized with a terrible craving to surrender thyself into my power. This must be such a great desire that you cannot eat nor sleep for it. It must be the craving of a man starving for food, or the man dying for thirst, or he who is suffocating for the want of air. It must be the only thing in thy thoughts.

"What doest thou care if thy body is clothed with rags, or thy stomach empty of food, if I have charge of thee, thy mind, and body? Thou must be emptied of everything to give me thy love, and I then will give thee life.

"Thou has beaten thy head against the wall, cried unbrokenly through the long nights, pleaded with God to come; but these all did not bring me to thee. For only by surrender can I come to take charge of thee.

"For I am God, thy Soul and mind!"

The seeker listened in amazement.

A Question on God

he wind ruffled the willows and whipped up the surface of the river. The Tibetan walked slowly along the bank studying the sunlight that glistened upon the water, and the seeker followed, watching every movement of the magnificent figure in his maroon robe.

"Sire," said the seeker, "tell me about God. What of Him? Is it true that one becomes God if he follows you?"

The majestic head nodded, and those deep, wise eyes gazed out across the broad water toward the far, wooded shores and round hills. "It is every man's destiny to become the Spirit of God," his deep voice rolled. "God is no-thing. But you cannot believe that God is no-thing. In your imagination, you create ideals and idols, and believe they are God.

"No! They are not God!

"They are only the attributes of God, for once you transcend time and space, beyond all creation, you meet with perfection.

"You find in the end that perfection is no-thing and no-thing is perfection. This is the SUGMAD, God!

"Therefore, seek nothing but God, and then you are seeking no-thing. Do I speak in riddles?

"Yes, I speak as such, for the seeking of God is to go beyond all the five worlds into the nameless region

19

where dwells the deity, the Absolute Father of all!

"There is no philosophy greater than that of the ECK. For in being one with the Spirit of God, thy Soul returns to God. This is entering into the true Kingdom of God. Surely, young sire, you do not yet know the true kingdom.

"Then I shall tell thee. The true kingdom is that world beyond all worlds, the Ocean of Love and Mercy, the Absolute Reality. It is so far above all mankind that the very ken of thought cannot even imagine what it might be. Seek nothing but the true kingdom, for it is the great void of all. The realm of God.

"Wayfarer, God has many levels of spiritual attainment, but concern thyself only with the true Home. Be not afraid to see God, for in desiring God thou hast true desire!

"So simple is life that man overlooks the truth of truths. The true disciple of God is he who has God. He who is a simple man. If you have God thus, it is true that you have a simple nature. Praise God, and love thy fellowman. Do all things in the name of the SUGMAD, without expecting rewards.

"Look to God for thy sustenance. What more does a man need in life?

"Thy virtues consist of steadfastness, love, and praise. Ah, there, dear one, you find the truths within the truth.

"The true teacher has transcended the state in which he is concerned for his own salvation. Then he is committed to the eternal welfare of all living beings, and will not rest until he has led them all to the true Home again.

"On attaining enlightenment, the teacher is commanded by God not to enter into the highest kingdom, but to remain in the world like any ordinary mortal and devote his spiritual skills to the aid of all Souls.

"He must now bear the duty of gathering up Souls for their return to their true Home, while acting in loving union with all beings, creation, worlds, and God.

"Joy, even-mindedness, bliss, and happiness are his rewards. He dwells with God while his feet walk the earth. Like the lotus flower, though it grows in the muddy water, is not polluted by the mud; so he, though born in this world, is not polluted by worldly things or desires.

"There is the answer. The law of God compels man to see Him, and you must know that even though you may never seek God, He will seek you and compel you to turn to Him.

"So I tell you this: Do as I say, and you shall become one with God! Do you see?"

Rebazar Tarzs stood quietly smiling down into the seeker's face. The wind skipped briskly across the water, and rattled the cattails and the willow branches.

The Tibetan laughed softly, and the seeker laughed with him.

The River of God

he thunderheads began to gather in the blue sky above the far mountains, and the leaves on the trees hanging over the waters of the river turned backward in a sudden gust of wind. Thunder growled and lightning ran through the white clouds above the snowy peaks.

The seeker sat under a large oak tree watching the river—the river ever flowing past to the sea, while its brown waters lap at the sandy shores with a murmuring sound.

"It is like the River of God," he said hopefully. "Will I ever see the great River which John spoke of in Revelation?"

Rebazar Tarzs said, "You shall see and know the glorious River of God, the Absolute. I shall take thee there to see God in His majestic glory!"

"Take me? Where shall we go?" asked the seeker in awe.

"Beyond the worlds of God's cosmic space. Into the far reaches of those spiritual regions where the foot of man has never trod, and where only Soul can journey. We will go where time, space, imagination, and ideas have no existence. Where only the true reality abides. That is where you shall see the River of God, flowing out of the divine throne!"

"How will we go?" asked the seeker eagerly.

"Just close thine eyes, and look into the Spiritual Eye. Wait for me to come. Then I shall take thee into the glorious sight of the divine River of God!"

The seeker closed his eyes and looked minutely into the Spiritual Eye between his brows. Gradually out of the darkness came the flowing rain of misty, yellow light, which enveloped him in a swirling cloud. With it came a strange humming sound like a thousand bees swarming through his head.

The light suddenly swirled fiercely and stopped, and he seemed to have a strange feeling of something happening to his body. A sucking sound, a motion, occurred at the top of his head, and there was a pop like a cork from a bottle, and he seemed to be lifted upward in a grand swoop. Surprised, he stopped, and stood looking at the body sitting on the ground. He said in amazement, "That is me!"

Then he looked at himself and saw the body he wore was something like a white sheath. The Tibetan was standing only a few feet away in similar attire.

"Soul," the Master explained. "It is dressed like this. You have now dropped the Physical, Astral, and Mental bodies. We stand at the top of the three worlds ready to

26

make the flight into the highest. You will know nothing, see nothing until you are ready for it.

"Take my hand. Have faith. I will show thee the River of God!"

The seeker closed his eyes and held tight to the Master's hand, and they seemed to fly through space. Within a matter of moments he heard his companion's voice say to open his eyes.

He was astounded. They seemed to be standing on the top of a vast wide tableland, overlooking a long valley in a dazzling white world. In the distance was a white, round circle that gleamed with wondrous brightness, and its distance from them could have been a hundred miles, or a thousand, he could not tell. Out of it poured a white, molten stream of Light so bright that he could hardly look at It, and this Light spread into the worlds becoming like rain falling upon the cosmic lands of God.

"There is God," said the Tibetan, pointing to the white disk in the great sky. "Out of God comes the River of Light; see It flowing into the Ocean of Mercy and Love. You cannot go any closer or you would die, for God will not let anything of imperfection approach Him.

"As the river is made of drops of water, so the River of God is made of the pure atoms which circulate throughout the worlds of God, down to the top of the three worlds. Then It returns to God, still pure in Its form.

"However, below the three worlds, and to the physical region, the stream of light travels as impure light, and eventually becomes a circle in which it keeps moving through its creator at the top of the three worlds. However, in time the stream does flow back to the center of that circle you see yonder, so as to be purified again.

"The Soul that has been gathered up by the divine hand of God, through the Guru, will use the Light for lighting the way so he can avoid the pitfalls, and the Sound as the current upon which to ride through to his true Home again.

"That is the light which you see when you are in contemplation!"

"Now you have seen and must go back!"

The seeker closed his eyes again. Upon reopening them, he found the Master and himself sitting by the river, in a gentle rain. The Master moved under the tree, and moved his hands with a familiar gesture.

"You see," he said in a most gentle voice, "I can give you the experience that you desire!"

The seeker nodded, looking at the black thunderclouds rolling up over the hills. Whitecaps were moving across the surface of the river. He smiled back at the Tibetan.

The Philosophy of All

ebazar Tarzs took off his sandals and placed them beside himself on the riverbank. Smiling, he looked across the broad waters at the gleaming riverpoint where a large bird fished. The seeker followed his glance and took in all the summer beauty of the river, and the Kashmir hills beyond.

The Traveler said, "Your spirit bears a heavy load, O seeker. Your conscience is deeply burdened. Only I can relieve you. Come and let me take your load!

"The worlds are sustained by my light and moved by my music. Man lives by the mercy of God's word. No creation of the light can exist except through the body of God. Only God can give life.

"The Spiritual Traveler is like a tree with its branches. The trunk represents the Traveler and the branches are his disciples. A Master who is without disciples is that tree which has no branches, and there can hardly be any branches without the trunk of the tree.

"I cannot give my love to those with the fly-bitten mind. When man is in the presence of those with such attitudes, he is bound fast to earthwise laws and codes that have nothing to do with God. The fly-bitten speak of God as if on intimate terms. But that sincerity rings with false notes. He desires to use God for his own selfishness, but alas, it is only a dream. Take him away—

for we have nothing to share!

"Now, know this. God is all. You cannot believe that God is all. In your imagination, you have and create ideals and idols, and then believe that is God. They are only the attributes of God; for once you transcend time and space, beyond all creation, you meet perfection and find in the end that perfection is all, and all is perfection.

"This is God.

"Do not partake of the evil of another. If you are quiet and calm, your calmness and quietness will make a greater effect on the other than his anger — so that true resistance is the practice of contentment.

"One who has not had the taste of God does not know His sweetest nectar of heavenly bliss.

"Who shall say what proportions of fact, past or present or to come, may lie in the imagination? But what is imagination? It is only the shadow of intangible truth. It is Soul's thought.

"Behold thy lot, O man. You live like a flame in the wind, snuffed out in the first gusty draft. Time after time, you live and sleep to be reborn again. Certainly you shall awake and live again, and again shall sleep through all the periods of time until the world is dead and the worlds beyond are your home, and finally you go to your true place in Spirit to live throughout eternity.

If thou slay good in thy self, I say unto thee that thou shalt not be in my holy memory and shall pluck no fruit from the ancient tree of love. What think thee? How will thee, man, take love from he who has loved and cherished thee?

"As long as thou art absorbed in thine own self, arising from inner conflict, there is no way of gaining victory over pain, or release from numbing bitterness of spiritual loss. You may gradually forget, as most people do, but that is to accept the numbness rather than folly, to adjust to reality.

"If, instead, one can identify in feeling with the experience of others who have similarly suffered, thou wilt be freed from thine own grief, or inner conflict, by and in a compassionate oneness with all living beings. This oneness intrinsically brings enduring peace and joy that are superior to inner strife. Superior because they do not spring from hopelessly trying to evade its cause or stoically steering the mind to its impact, but through overcoming evil to one's self by the good of a deep and satisfactory love for others."

The Tibetan finished and sat in the sunlight that spread its great golden light across the sparkling river. He picked up the sandals and put them on again, then rose from the ground and went down to the river to drink from his hands.

The seeker watched silently, wondering at the wisdom of the cosmic Traveler.

Love

cold wind ruffled the willows. Rags of clouds went racing through the dark sky. The moon sailed through the heavens in and out of banks of clouds, gleaming upon the river flowing through the fertile lands.

The seeker pulled his cloak around himself and looked at the Tibetan who walked aimlessly along the bank where the waters lapped in a melody of sounds.

"Ah, Sire, how I love thee in the softness of the night," he said. "I look into the moon and see thy face sleeping there. Thou art in my beloved, and thou art in my heart. Never leave me. Never!"

"Look to me, thy Guide, for love," said Rebazar Tarzs. "Only I can give thee peace and comfort of the spirit!"

"Then love me, Sire, and give me rest!"

The Traveler smiled gently. "Have patience, my son. Have patience though the world strikes and strains at thy temper. Ah, you know that happiness is the greatest thing in thy life. But I say that all disagreement between thy friends and thee comes from impatience. If you have patience, then life will teach thee better."

"Speak to me of love, O Master!"

Rebazar Tarzs again smiled. "Love is desire, and

desire is feeling. Therefore, when you have a deep feeling, you have desire for something!

"Love is absolute. But the conception of love varies with the individual consciousness. No man can say when the individual consciousness has been developed to the point where further unfoldment is impossible.

"Love is not a matter of belief. It is a matter of demonstration. It is not a question of authority, but one of perception and action.

"The requirements of growth demand that you exert the greatest degree of love for what is perfectly in accord with Soul. Our highest happiness will be best attained through our understanding of, and conscious cooperation with, the divine law.

"It is love that imparts vitality to our minds and hearts and enables it to germinate. The law of love will bring to you all necessity for your spiritual growth and maturity.

"Therefore, if you desire love, try to realize that the only way to get love is by giving love. That the more you give, the more you get; and the only way in which you can give is to fill yourself with it, until you become a magnet of love.

"God love has for its goal the creation of the highest form, and you must know that the individual love is likewise forever attempting to express itself in form, and to give Soul the highest architecture of spiritual attainment.

"Open thine eyes, O man, and look steadily for love. Then you will learn the secrets as have I; the bright angel of the true Home will stand before you in a glorious robe. He will give you the secrets of love as never before imparted. But be cautious, my curious one, for it is dangerous to look for the angel of love unless you are filled with sincerity. He can blind you or make you great.

"If you are able to see love in its entirety, you will know all things, the all in all, the secrets of all reality. If not, you will be chained to this old world of darkness and suffering forever!

"When I have gone from thee, my chosen one, when at night thou stretchest out thy hand and cannot find me, then thou shouldst think of what glories might have been thine. For of a truth, I love thee well, though ye are not yet fit to wash my feet, but I am of the humble state to bow before thee, and wash thy feet.

"Now let us love and take that which belongs to thee, and be happy. Tonight is now and the moment is now, for eternity is in this very moment.

"A kiss from the Lord enters into the scheme of life. His kisses often leave no scars except upon the heart. But if thou doest not kiss the hem of the Lord's robe, then how can the Lord return thy kiss?

"I tell thee of a surety if this is not done you shall eat out thy heart for the love of the Lord and die.

"There, my son, is love. The love that makes all things beautiful. Yes, and breathes divinity into the very dust you tread. With love shall life roll on gloriously throughout eternity, like the voice of great music that has power to hold the hearer's heart poised on eagle's wings far above the earthly world."

He ended and moved off into the darkness among the fairy willows which swayed in the cold winds. The seeker rose to follow him.

The Beloved

he seeker sat in the darkness while the wind blew around him and his beloved, and the river sang its way past into the flat plains of India.

He kept wondering if God had put him and this woman together, sitting silently side by side. But he knew that whether God meant it or not, he would soon be gone.

He wondered where the Tibetan might be out there in the darkness; probably wandering about with his mind upon the universal work.

The seeker's thoughts returned to the girl, and over and over the thought ran through his mind, "We are one. Nothing I say or do can be kept from her."

His hand reached up and touched her hair, and then suddenly he looked at her with the starlight in her eyes.

Then as suddenly as his thoughts had begun, they stopped that very moment, and the world stood still.

He pulled away and looking up saw Rebazar Tarzs standing beside them, his right hand raised in blessing. He said, "Shall it be life or shall it be death? Yet death is only the night of life, for out of the night comes the morning. Only when day and night and life are one, and swallowed up in that from which they came, shall

43

ye both have at-one-ment with God and with thy own two selves."

The seeker said, "Long have we waited for thee, O Lord. Yet our love for thee lessened not. Long have we waited, and now our reward is at hand. We sought thee once far away, and thou left us alone. Now through the hours of the night we have struggled to reach thee, and have found thee again at our side. Therefore, we rejoice for the Light is with us, and the Sound in us, and thou art before us."

"Reach to me, my beloved ones," said the Traveler. "Reach to me across the gulf of time. Put your hand upon mine, and I will lead thee to God. To the Absolute Father who is all-present, all-powerful, and all-knowing!"

Taking their hands in his, he seated himself on the ground and said, "Behold the hawk in the sky. It sails with the wind, gliding upon the air currents looking for its victim. Are ye immortal against the talons of the hawk? Yet ye live upon the strong bread of this earth. No, ye must turn to the Lord for tender nurture and strength to endure life.

"Ah, man, you have profaned thy woman. Forgive me, God, but man has all but broken woman by his careless entanglement of her heart and abandonment of her love. Ah, but let me look into the heart of woman and see the love she has for man, her husband, son or lover. It is only the reflection of thy love, O God!

"Woman, your lamp cannot burn without oil; and man cannot live without woman. Neither of ye can live without one another nor without God! He alone is really a great Soul who is illuminated with spiritual light!

"Strength, beauty, power, and all the things dear to man are but bubbles. Is not ambition but an endless ladder by which no heights are climbed until the last unreachable rung is mounted? Heights lead but to heights, and there is no resting place upon the rungs, for rungs grow upon rungs and there is no limit to the number. Life becomes dull and no longer serves to satisfy hours of pleasure, or to buy an ease of mind.

"Is there no end to wisdom, my children, so that ye may hope to win it? Is not thy wisdom but a gnawing hunger calling thy consciousness day by day to a knowledge of the empty craving of the mind? Would it then not be better to serve the Lord for a tiny crumb from His table? Whereby man could have just a glimpse of God's face rather than none? Nay, I tell thee, my children, it is time for man's hunt for God; he seeks God everywhere but where I really am!

"Where do I really dwell, O man? I will tell thee. In the heart of thy beloved. Look there and see me, my son!

"So I tell thee, my children, this great principle. Human love is that which speaks of the self; a selfish love which demands a return of the love that pours forth.

"And divine love is that which has no thought of anything in return. When ye both have the love of others, regardless of what may happen or be done to thee, then ye have divine love.

"When ye love one another so great that it does not matter what the other does, then ye have unconditional love, and thy love has risen above the planes of this earthly world.

"Then ye know how to love me, thy God and Creator."

The Guru dropped their hands and arose, looking down into the darkness, his great black eyes shining with fire through the shadows. Then he turned and strolled toward the murmuring river, a majestic figure in the windy night.

Life

he pattern of light fell through the leaves of the great oak, covering the seeker as he looked out across the grass at the girl wading in the shallow edge of the river, and nearby the Traveler was watching.

There were moments in his life when the seeker seemed to reach the heights of ecstasy.

Something he saw struck an accord within him. The sunlight was lying sweetly across the fields, and the world of the river and snowcapped mountains seemed emptied, yet occupied.

He was at peace and inwardly he was filled with joy, for this was God, God the beautiful!

He said, "O Sire, to know, to be, to have, and to seek is the answer of what I am after. I will give up all to get that. Is it God? How do I know? All I can say is that it is an inner longing to have. To be."

The Tibetan replied. "You seek to become a law unto thyself. You wish to be responsible to nobody but God. When you reach — when you become one with the Spirit of God — then you will live only according to the workings of the inner law."

"Sire, I have walked the night looking for thee. I have looked into the faces of children in strange lands and talked with the priests of unknown worlds. I looked for thee in the sunset in the far Pacific, and in Tibet where ice and snow rule the land.

"I spoke to the world, Sire; I called for thee in the country of Tibet. I pleaded with thee to take me with thee. I have lived in agony. Dost thou want me to wither away on this earthly plane? Wilt thou not tell me what might be the truth? The world of light?"

The girl was looking at them with an intensity. When the Tibetan motioned, she bounded forward like a deer, and stood beside him with downcast eyes.

"I will tell thee this. I will speak to thee in riddles.

"The leopard is hungry but he cannot seize his food for the deer is swifter. So my friend, there is man who is also hungry in spirit for my word, and whose boasting roar does not bring me nearer to him.

"Neither can man nor the leopard lie in wait to seize Spirit. No, ye can do nothing.

"The leopard is the lord of the jungle, so I am told. Is it the monarch of the animal kingdom? Then tell me, does it conquer the elephant? Can it outwit the fox, outrun the deer? No, then it is not the king of the jungle for it rules by fear.

"So he who rules without love will die. And I tell thee that all thy vanity is in vain. You shall seek me through all incarnations until you are man, and then a Master.

"Ah, now, my friends, ye are like the leopard. Ye have such self-esteem. And what great pain it brings for you. Shake thy little self like the dog shakes its bone, and tell it to go away. Now ye listen. That self-esteem is but thy ego hiding in the brush behind thy vanity and impatience. Be of good cheer for we shall send it away.

"The SUGMAD is the center of all things, and there thy mind must dwell at all times; ye must put thy faith in me, the Master. Thus, I repeat what Seneca, the Roman said, 'The greatest man is he who chooses right with invincible determination.'

"The heart must be willing and aspire to serve God through love. By this joyful performance, the heart fulfills God's great principle of love, and becomes known through the worlds of God; for none can withhold himself from love.

"The upturned face of the furrowed clod is the work of the Lord. He is there within the lowly worm, and ye are also in that tiny creature. So do not become proud and believe that it is only thyself who is of God. Then, I will speak in the double tongue—thou art not God, not the lowly worm, but nothing.

51

"Ah, now look not confused, for this is only the play of maya with words. God is the power, the all-intelligent and the all-present. These are the attributes of God—not God ITSELF, or Himself. The true reality is the source of God. Therefore, to become one with God ye must become a part of the true source, and not the power.

"Therefore, thy at-one-ment with God is becoming the instrument for His power, and not God ITSELF. To become one with God, thou must return to the true Home as Soul. This is life!

"You see?"

Smiling, the Tibetan held up two fingers and walked down to the sandy shore of the murmuring river. The seeker turned and looked into the eyes of the girl beside him and saw her love shining brightly.

The Eternal Principles

he river gurgled and sung its way past the shore. A tree loomed darkly against the night sky. Its branches opened enough to show the seeker a star shining brilliantly through the foliage.

The essence of what he saw struck fire in his mind for a brief moment, and his inner vision opened like a white light showing the worlds upon worlds.

A strange joy burst in his Soul and his blood turned to wine that sparkled and danced through his veins. Looking up he saw the Tibetan approaching in the dark and come to a halt beside him.

"Sire," said the seeker, "you are the one whom I have long sought. You are the essence of my happiness."

"Ah, young one," replied the Traveler, "the worlds turn within thee. Thou art the little world within the great world. Seek only God, and nothing else!"

"I love thee, Sire!"

Rebazar Tarzs smiled. "All words are symbols of hidden meanings. The divine power is a hidden meaning which includes unseen forces that daily shape man's life. You are like the fish that live in the sea. Obey God, or suffer!"

"Speak to me, O Sire, and give me thy wisdom," the seeker begged.

"You radiate divine intelligence and peace to the world because you are an individualization of God. The scriptures speak of the birth of Christ as the babe being born of the virgin. Any divine idea arising in the mind or Soul is that which comes out of the great sea of God's Ocean of Mercy and Love, and, therefore, is a God-given idea for the good of all mankind.

"God is life; therefore, God is existence, and God is consciousness. These are the attributes of God. Existence is that eternal reality in which dwells all creation.

"The love of God can give you the glorious heights that thereby help you overcome all things of this world. It exists because of this, the existence of all reality.

"So I tell you, my son, that the secret of true happiness is for him who asks nothing in return. The perfectly unselfish man is the one who finds his glory in God. Give what you have to give, and it will come back to you. All materials to build thy home in this world or the inner cosmic worlds come from within, from the God center in thy heart.

"Therefore, love all with kindness, understanding, forgiveness, and with the oneness of Soul with God."

"The experience of contentment or delight itself is located in the process of relaxation. It must contain an awareness of coming out of some turmoil or struggle. When changes cease, we suffer a distress of emptiness and we turn to another project, as Soul, in the seeking of God. Thus, I say, we do not discontinue the goal but look, seek, and understand God with a great depth, and deeper penetration of the mind, heart, and Soul.

"So I tell you this, the three eternal principles of ECKANKAR are the proper understanding of God, a knowledge of God, and a knowledge of the creation by God.

"Understand these three principles and thou art great in the sight of the True Holy Father."

"This I promise you. If you seek within to find the God center, thy ideal can be fulfilled. It depends upon thyself, for every man is the truth and the way unto himself. Speaking to his disciples, Jesus said, 'I am the way and the truth,' but he was speaking from the Christ consciousness and not as Jesus, the man.

"So I speak to thee, my son, from the highest, from the plane of God, and not as an individual. God is thy own for the asking. You need no man, except the Master, to show thee. Mainly, you need thyself to make it a reality.

"The more you are aware that the Light of God centers you, the more you will become aware that the Light is thy very self, and that thy body is but an extension of thy self which was created to manifest thy self.

"The more that awareness grows, the more you become the cosmic being, and the more you know. When you finally become fully aware of that supreme being as thyself, you are that supreme being.

"Let us leave off here."

He finished and gazed at the dark murmuring river. The heaven reflecting in the water was like a fisherman's net full of gold.

"Good night," said the Tibetan abruptly and walked off.

The seeker murmured an answer, sitting in the darkness of the tree. His Soul seemed to have suddenly become free, an experience of relaxing, the coming out of the darkness into the light.

Suddenly he felt spiritually free, and sat there in the night listening to the singing river.

The Law of the Self

he seeker moved along the riverbank restlessly wondering at his state of mind. The great stream flowed past murmuring its song in a beautiful melody, washing against the sandy shore.

Boats moved along the broad surface of the river, while the brilliant sunlight glistened upon the water dripping from slushing wheels. Melodious whistles echoed in the high hills, and far down the shore he saw the levee where the white, graceful boats were pushed against the docks and men moved busily loading them.

He turned to the Guru and said, "Can you think of life to be no more than what it is this moment? When the pattern of love and joy rushes into this world of mine to find it empty?

"In the night I found my beloved sleeping by my side dreaming of a world lightly touched with love. Gently she felt my hand that touched her and pressed it to her side. Can life be no more than this, O Master? Tell me, my teacher!"

The great river with its sounds of flowing water and dreamy noise of whistles went through his mind as though a part of himself. He saw the land that lay with the gallant misty blue haze across the mountains and shores.

The Tibetan said, "Ah, you seek the higher self, through ECK. Thy first individual desire is always the determinative factor in thy experience. The first cause of all creative thinking and God-seeking is the initial choice of thought. The initial choice of thought creates its own Godlike circumstances and conditions. Thy experience is nothing less than thy own choices and thoughts made visible. The creative order of God is always moving from the spiritual plane to the mental into circumstances and conditions."

"Yes, Sire, but today I caught a glimpse of that great Oversoul in entirety. I have seen the struggle of mankind and the very control of their earth world destiny by individuals who have control of their lives and the power currents."

Smiling the Tibetan replied, "Thy vision has overlooked the fact that Soul is mightier than space, stronger than time, deeper than the sea, and higher than the stars.

"The word of God is bread and wine for the struggling. No man can hold his fellowman under his petty self, for some day God appears and then all the little desires and willpowers of the lower self are dried up like a puddle of water in the hot sunlight. Those who have been withheld from God go forward to Him, and the Soul who had the control must learn a lesson.

"Thus, I am a stranger to man in this world, and he looks not to me, but to the gaining of power. Yet I love this world. So, I ask you, my son, what spiritual food have you stored up for thy journey into the worlds beyond after you leave this world?

"Now I speak to thee in riddles. But to the ears of those who can hear the truth, nothing I say is a riddle. My words are the truth and are timeless. There is nothing ordinary about the word of God, and to the seekers of God I speak the word of God. Therefore, I say, any words spoken in the name of God give the message of the divine cause. So listen and understand.

"Be content and let thy mind go like the river you see before thine eyes, which is always flowing onward, forever to the ocean, and yet is untouched by anything.

"Life is like that river—a continuation, birth upon birth, and death upon death. Only indifference acts as the separating influence. Neither love nor hate, but remain self-contained, living inwardly always for God.

"You, yourself, are your own problem. You must understand and act to solve the mystery of thy little self before you can solve the mystery of God. This is the law of the Self—the law of God. Therefore, I tell you not to take up the seeking of God until the little self within thee is conquered and solved.

"Do not lay claim to salvation as long as gossip still appeals to thee; so long as you are more disturbed by the faults of others than by thine own; so long as you can still excuse thine own weakness and shift thine own blame to another, you have not settled thy problem of the little self."

Rebazar Tarzs said again, "I am someone from thy past, now settled in thee. Do not be afraid. I am a part of thy self. My wisdom is beyond the conception of the mortal senses. Learn ECK, it is the true way. Be wise and follow the path of ECK."

The silence fell around them, and the river water lapped softly at the shores in a gentle music that penetrated the seeker's Soul, going deeper and deeper into that mystic center of his heart.

Sermon by the River

man came to the river and seated himself before Rebazar Tarzs. Another followed, and still another, until there came a multitude who bowed and seated themselves.

And the seeker looked at them and turned to the Tibetan saying, "They have heard of thy wisdom and wish to hear thee speak."

A thin, ragged man stood up and spoke. "Yes, speak to us, great Soul. Give us a crumb of thy wisdom of that merciful One whom we seek."

"Man is always seeking," the Guru replied smiling. "And he finds not, for life does not begin with birth and end with death. Man hungers after perfection. Man seeks God. And how can man find God, without the Godman's help, in twenty, a hundred, or a thousand years? If ye are dead, He will bring thee back again to seek Him. Again He will cause thee to die, and shall bring ye back again. But in the end He shall gather all Souls and then take ye into His kingdom."

"I had a dream of thee, great Soul," said the ragged man. "What was this dream of thee that came in the night when my face was lifted to the sky? I asked God where was His son; and now I find thee."

Smiling, Rebazar Tarzs said, "We have all met

before. Centuries ago under a banyan tree ye all sat listening to my words. In many lands, here in this earth world and in the beyond we have been together, and shall always be together in thy long journey to reach God's eternal goal.

"Life is but a perpetual balancing of accounts. Man dies leaving behind many unsettled accounts. Some are debits, some are credits; man is debited with the evil he does and credited with the good he does. Therefore, he must return again to this world to pay and collect. And he shall come and go until the ECK Master appears and gathers him up for God.

"The true value of life is to be humble before all God's creatures. The greatness of God and need for humility leads to a pure and honest life, for an ethical life is but a stepping-stone to spirituality. Did not thy great teacher Jesus say that except ye become as little children, ye shall not enter into the Kingdom of God?

"Love for thy fellow creatures as the children of God makes ye not only true to thyself but also true to thy village and to all humanity at large within this earth world, and those citizens of the seven spheres beyond. This leads to the expansion of Soul, and ye become a conscious Co-worker of God, with a cosmopolitan outlook on life.

"The eternal truth of the seven heavens of the cosmic universe is that God is one. What we call this divine reality is only our name for it. But all races and countries have a different name, and even the sages and rishis called it by their own name. Yet, it is the same in any language. Only he who has experienced this reality in God can present with authority its various facets of truth and give a true import of the conflicting views of the various scriptural texts.

"Make love thy master, for love is God, and whosoever loves God shall love that which we call love. It is love that binds thee to God, and it is love which unbinds thee from evil and sets thy feet upon the path of righteousness. Love is absolute and a law unto itself.

"To have freedom ye must seek God, for only He can give thee that which unbinds the chains of this world and lifts the Spirit into the true kingdom. Freedom is that in which Soul dwells in ecstasy in an infinity where the self is merged into one all-embracing, boundless Self.

"Ye are the same Spirit of God which moved upon the face of the water when the earth was without form and void, and darkness was upon the face of the deep. From whence comes the joy when God stirs within thee? Are ye not the earth itself, and the Soul of thy fellowman? Search within thyselves and see what God has brought thee in the everlasting world of the cosmic self. Ye belong beyond time and space and in that world of the nameless one that ye call God.

"There is no dividing line between thyselves and anything else throughout the seven spheres of God. If thy fellowman suffers, thou must suffer with him, and thou must share his joy also.

"Ye have been blessed, people of the river, for the keys to the kingdom have been given thee this day!"

With that the great head dropped and his chin rested on his chest. The Tibetan's eyes closed as if in silent worship of God. Beside him the seeker studied the majestic composure of the face with reverence.

Slowly and silently the multitude of people arose and drifted away into the gray bank of fog that was lifting over the land and water in a dense sheet of heavy, whirling vapor.

The Mirror of God

heavy gray mist closed in around the small city, and the people who passed Rebazar Tarzs and his chela were like ghostly wraiths coming out of the curling wisps. The seeker and his Guru walked steadily toward the river in the distance.

The continued echoing of whistles from the steamers sounded deeply against the curtains of mist which hid the rising sun of the morning. Other sounds were lost in the heavy gray fog.

Finally the two reached the riverbank and the seeker threw his package of food upon the grass under the giant oak and started looking for twigs to build a fire. Soon he had a blaze merrily gleaming in the dripping mist. As he opened the package to prepare food for eating, he said, "I suppose that God is like a mirror. I would say the Mirror of God. And anything that stands before it will be reflected without any reason from the mirror."

Smiling the Tibetan replied, "That is right. But you speak of the universal body of God, not of God ITSELF. Anything that is beautiful, ugly, rich or poor, good or bad, all in all is reflected by that mirror. It is impartial to all that stands before it—and all the worlds of space and time are affected by this mirror. It is like the fog that echoes the sound of the steamers' whistles because it cannot penetrate the deep curtain of mist!"

"I think that I understand about the mirror, but not about how it reflects all situations, circumstances, and actions, O Master."

"Ye speak of karma, my son," said the Tibetan gazing deeply into the blazing fire. "All particular things are reflected in the body of God—that is the mind and matter body of God. Everything below in the three worlds is a part of the law of God called karma. The mirror reflects all deeds and actions, in this part of the heavenly spheres, without hesitation and without reason."

The seeker studied his thoughts a moment, and said, "Ye have said that all obstacles thrown in the path of the devotee and all traps laid for him are the result of the Universal Mind Power."

"Yea," the Master smiled, " 'tis true. Any trap or obstacle laid by mind and matter which stops or interferes with the progress of the devotee who is striving to reach the highest mansion of God will disappear at once upon the declaration of the sacred names of God.

"Yea, and let me say that anyone who fights with evil should be careful lest he thereby become evil itself. For if you look too long into the mirror with eyes that see only evil, then the reflection will be that of evil and thine own self will be filled with evil.

"All life is one; therefore, there cannot be God and man, nor universes. All things are in God and must return to Him, and He operates in all things. He is the creator, and the created. Thus all is God, and God is all. So I tell you not to believe, but understand; and not to worship, but to practice. Do you see?

"So I say to you that everyone who looks into the Mirror of God shall see the exact likeness of himself, be it good or bad. That is so long as he remains below in the three worlds. But once he transcends the top of the three worlds, by the path of ECKANKAR, he is beyond all good and bad—beyond all relativity where Soul is neither punished nor rewarded.

"Karma then is the underlying principle of personal responsibility. All actions and reactions are equal, but opposite in nature. It is the governing power in the kingdom of mind and matter.

"Pure Spirit governs the higher worlds. There is no karma there, for the higher law—the law of love—supersedes all other laws.

"Now you must understand. Every man seeking to balance the law of God should seek first to render a service for what he expects to get. This is the law of this world and must never be broken.

"To get the proper perspective of what you see in the mirror, you must have a pure heart. Then you can see God, for God is thine own self and you are God.

"So remember that to live in life immersed in joy, as does the fish in the river, is the highest of all attributes of God in this world. Then you will see thine own true reflection in the Mirror of God!"

The seeker stared into the leaping flames wrapped in deep thought. A curtain of fog lifted suddenly, and the long shafts of sunlight lay across the Guru's feet.

The Loving Heart

sharp touch of frost in the evening air made the seeker pull his cloak around himself. The sky was so thick with stars that it had the effect of moonlight showering the river. The scarlet-and-gold leaves dropped from the trees steadily upon the earth.

The seeker and the girl walked slowly along the bank of the river examining this ever-changing world, and watching the river that flowed past, forever toward the sea. He watched the petite girl walking before him along the path, and thought that the rhythm of her step was different from other women.

When he gazed upon her, his heart danced for she was beautiful with God. Her voice was the voice of the river, the whispering of the wind and the rustle of the autumn leaves dropping upon the age-old land.

She said, "The longing for God draws back the curtain that hides the mystery of God, and from the fragments of wisdom that compose understanding we know that nothing, no other understanding, can surpass what is in our hearts and Souls."

"Can it be that the search for God is that of two divine Souls together?" the seeker asked. "Or is it an alliance of two beings so strong in love that all the angels in heaven rejoice in its purity? Do we have a golden link in that invisible cord of love that stretches throughout all eternity?"

"I do not know," she said.

Then they saw the maroon-robed figure of the Traveler standing among the trees. He came forward and spoke, "Ah, I must speak with thee, my friends. This is the night to tell thee of the loving heart.

"Ye know that the greatest of God's qualities is love. For love is the greatest and most sublime force of the universe. Through love the divine qualities of God will shine like the radiant light of the morning sun.

"I will whisper to thee, dear ones, this divine secret. Let thine ears become filled with wisdom and thy hearts with understanding. Now it is this: All things will gravitate to thee if ye will let love enter thine own hearts, without compromise.

"By obeying this command of God, ye become an inspiration and beauty to all thy fellow creatures, even though some may never hear of thee again. So I say that to serve and cherish love as an ideal is as unquestionable as the tender fragrance of the autumn flowers that grow upon the shores of yon river.

"So it is the Lord's command that ye look into thine own hearts and see if purity dwells there. If ye find this to be true, then the Lord is with thee throughout all eternity.

"Love inspires the heart, first as human love. This is the love which desires to serve its beloved, husband, wife, children, family, friends, or human ideals, and the things of this world, during thy existence here in this life.

"Then the heart becomes refined by selflessness and love possesses thee."

Joy flooded through the seeker like water bursting over a fall, and ecstasy made a great shining light within him and burst wildly.

He held himself breathlessly, his eyes closed, witnessing the phenomena within himself.

Beyond Wisdom

he seeker sat silently beside the river. Darkness flowed around him like a current of wind while the autumn leaves dropped slowly to the earth in a lovely whisper of summer memory.

He watched the thoughts inside his mind. They came and went in strange movements, expanding like ocean waves, growing ever greater and moving outward into the unknown, into space and time far beyond his mind.

They would return in a roaring wave striking upon the shores of his mind like an ocean torn by a storm, and the suddenness of it would startle him. Yet fascinated, he was not the physical self, but some deep entity watching the strange mechanism of his body.

He knew that those waves of the mind came from only one place within himself: a center deep in his consciousness where he had never before visited. Suddenly he realized this was the dwelling place of Soul. It was like the discovery of another world, the likeness of which he had never before known.

Opening his eyes he looked at the dark singing river and saw the Tibetan seated by the shore. A chord of joy at finding that great Soul with him moved out of that deep center within and touched something within

Rebazar and returned. The return of it gave the seeker sudden, but extreme bliss.

"You are experiencing the ECK?" he smiled.

"I understand something," the seeker replied, shaking his head. "But what it is, I do not know!"

The Sat Guru smiled again. "You have experienced Soul within thyself. As long as man is immersed in emotional matter, as long as he is bound by the things of Samsara, his higher God energies will be poured into the external world instead of within himself. And when man is bound by that condition, he can go no higher, nor will he know his higher Self.

"Therefore, before you can enter into the Kingdom of Heaven, it is necessary that you balance the scale of harmony within thyself. So you see that when Soul has come to the last barrier between Itself and the pure state of God, It must drop the mind.

"As long as thy mind continues with thee in its present state, even the love for the beautiful, it is pouring its God energies into the external world and unbalancing Soul's forces. So I tell you to turn thy energies within and receive the blessings of God."

The seeker listened briefly to the singing waters beside him, then spoke. "Tell me, Sire, how does one reach that state beyond the self?"

"That state is beyond wisdom and beyond all but love." The Tibetan spread his hands. "I tell you this, when you have attained wisdom and gone beyond illusion, then you shall shine forth with splendor, as doth the sun shining upon the earth.

"You must give up thy mind and body, and enter into the heavenly kingdom in the pure body. There is no way to God except through the path of ECKANKAR, and there can be no denying of this.

"Nothing but the perfect bliss of God exists within the true, heavenly home. I have no words of glory to describe this state of heaven. It is glorious and peaceful to the Soul that dwelleth there, and none desire to return to this earth after a taste of the bliss of thy Lord. So you must seek nothing but this; and then again, I tell you not to seek it, for the Lord will not reward thee for thy deeds, for in this land there is no reward, no good nor evil. You must earn thy way into heaven by the casting off of all bondage within this world.

"Nothing can compare to His pure Light, and the result of encountering this Light will destroy all thy bonds of karma and give thee refuge in Him who lives in the Heaven of Heavens.

"Pain and suffering exists in the mind and body of man until he takes refuge in the omnipresence of God.

Until man decides to do this, he will continue to live in the duality of this world and cannot be drawn into his inner God-self, where the realization of all things of the seven spheres of heaven may be possible.

"Therefore I tell you that you must examine, inspect, and release all things in a state of balance, being swayed neither to the right, nor to the left, nor up, nor down. Then having learned to live in the center of Soul, you will rejoice in the perfect bliss of God.

"But until you learn to bring thy senses under subjection there can be no living in Soul, within thy holy self!"

The seeker saw the great smile on the Tibetan's lips and felt the joy of Soul rising within himself. He lifted his head and laughed with happiness, for suddenly everything in this world seemed to be filled with throbbing waves of rapture.

Rebazar Tarzs joined him, and their laughter rang out over the waters. The birds stirred in their nests and chirped sleepily, and even the fishes in the deep river stopped and listened with wondrous delight.

The Language of God

he seeker strolled through the high cattails along a beaten path overlooking the river. The deceptive, leonine waters lapped at the foot of a sandy embankment where the Tibetan sat with his feet in the water. The world was blue and gold, filled with a spring festival of flowers and greenery.

Stopping, he voiced his thoughts. "It is not necessary to read books anymore. By doing so I am voicing other people's ideas. All that is necessary now is to keep my mind on God. The realization is upon me now to be with God, to do nothing but live in God, and spend long hours dwelling on God."

"Yea, that is truth," replied Rebazar Tarzs, studying the movements of a cricket crawling along a blade of grass. "This earth's civilization has made man soft and flabby, and no longer can he think for himself. He must let others do so, tell him what to do. He is weak and fat in his protective environment."

"I think," said the seeker, "man has become so engrossed in living a life of ease that he has sacrificed health and vigor. If he had the endurance of the primitive, there would be a profound effect upon his spirit as well as the flesh!"

The Sat Guru smiled. "Man must regain his adventuresome spirit, and then he will want to live spiritually, boldly and dangerously. Then he will not be caught up in a great drive for security. Security? What security? Does anyone have security without God? Is not the greatest security the strength of Spirit?

"This is all because man has forgotten the language of the celestial world. God speaks to all, but how many hear His Voice? It comes from within man telling him what glories lie beyond this earth world; It also comes in the wind, the waters of this river, and through all the voices of nature and man.

"Man has become so involved in the trifles of existence that he is shut off from God. Therefore, Soul is forgotten and everything proceeding from It is so hazy that man's life has become a constant swaying between the poles of pain and pleasure. Yet the few who have come to see themselves in the true Light of God, and whose life is in keeping with the guidance of God, are rightfully named the Messengers of God, and are His Supreme Sons who give the truth to all mankind. They are the Godmen who walk the earth.

"So I tell you, do not despise man because he cannot see his true self, but give him compassion and mercy. He is blinded and must stay in this state until God has mercy upon him and sends a Saint to give him Light.

"Man cannot understand the celestial language. He has talked of God since time immemorial; and written of God ever since he learned the art of writing; and tried to catch some aspect or attribute of God in song, music, art, and sculpturing since his beginning in this world.

"But God remains invisible to the external eye, too magnificent to be caught in words, too majestic for song or music, and too vast and formless for pictures and statues. Why? Verily, I will tell thee the reason. It is because man has not learned the celestial language of God, not made any attempt to understand its true meaning. Those few who have done so are not noticed and have been soon forgotten, for man, as man, cannot understand.

"So I tell you that to reach ultimate wisdom is to realize the true nature of God. And once this is revealed to Soul, the tongue and hand cannot broadcast it, nor encase it in picture or statue.

"Then what is the essence of the true language of God? Silence is the keynote of the realization of that strange, holy communication which can guide thee back to the Kingdom of Heaven. So in human language, the nearest would be rendering the holy names of God in repetition to thyself.

"What else is there to say to thyself?"

"Can you utter Truth before Truth is uttered in thee as Soul? Do you obey Truth in thy mind? If so, then you should be able to utter nothing but Truth, and then you should have no need to preach Truth, but will demonstrate it in every aspect of thy life. As Jesus said, let thy light so shine before thee.

"The Soul that is free will radiate the Truth of God in its strange language of celestial demonstration. What you might call false cannot be so. For God has made all things of Himself, and therefore all things should be above the untrue. Only pure silence will lead to the freedom of Soul and the profound glory of God.

"When you see the glory of God, thy tongue will be speechless. You will no longer cling to the earth, and will live continuously in Paradise. And if you must speak, it will be couched in the majestic celestial language of the SUGMAD, the Almighty Father!"

The Tibetan lifted his feet from the water and started drying them on his robe. The cricket crept down on the end of the blade, as if curious to see what those broad hands were doing. It chirped twice, and the seeker looked at it in astonishment, wondering if the insect had understood.

The Celestial Word

ll was well this night with the seeker until the wind began to blow. He had finished his contemplation and talked with the Master. His life was in order as always, until the wind blew this night.

Yes, all was well, until this night when he stood by the dark, flowing river in a world where a burning star made a strange light over the hills and valleys and gleamed beautifully upon the water. It was then in the darkness from beyond the far shores he heard, the first time, the sound of the wind. It was a low sound, deep and humming, and seemingly a part of the darkness.

He raised his head and listened. He left off everything and stood there listening, and soon everything else was gone; his thoughts, his life, the starlit world; all gone and lost—and that was all there was, the darkness and the sound.

He turned to Rebazar Tarzs under the tree. "What is that strange sound like the wind, O Master? What might it be?"

"What you hear is of thy own true self, my son," the Sat Guru replied, pointing. "There is no wind. Look you yonder at the river and see there is no disturbance of the water!"

The seeker shook his head. "Strange, I believe that it is the wind. But it is a haunting melody which comes from the worlds beyond, a formless sound which cannot be fitted into any pattern. It makes me desire God."

"Tell me more of thy own feelings," the Master smiled. "What do you hear?"

"I am not sure what I hear. I listen and a wind hums, and the humming seems a thing of my own body and brain. But then it changes. It is outside me. It flows into me from the night over the city, the night over the land. It comes from some far-off distance, across the sea, a continent."

The Tibetan laughed. "Yea, and from the worlds beyond. What you hear is the Voice of God—the celestial Word which is that mighty spiritual current flowing forever out of the throne of God to sustain the worlds of cosmic creation.

"All men can hear It if they stop and listen. Only some more clearly than others. That is why you hear tonight—because thy spiritual ears are open. That is why you stand there listening to the Voice of God speaking from His great throne in the far beyond. He is calling for Soul to return to Its true Home. And Soul has heard and is yearning to go.

"The Voice of God is that Sound Current within the

cosmic body of the Lord, and within thy own body. Sometimes It is known as the five melodies, or by many names by various religions. St. John spoke of It in the Holy Bible.

"The Voice of God is man's divine link with the Almighty SUGMAD. Until you understand that the unceasing internal melody within thyself is the path over which to travel to reach the Eternal Home, then you will struggle in vain.

"It is the true Spirit Current and is like the great river yonder; for if you try to divert it one way, then it flows another. Stop it and it will overflow the banks. So it is better to open thy spiritual ears and listen to the Music of the seven spheres as It flows through thee. Open thyself, thy heart and Soul to It, unafraid and gladly.

"So I tell you that it is necessary to have both the Light and Sound in thy spiritual life. The Light is for the traveling Soul to see the pitfalls and obstructions on Its journey to God, and the Sound is for Soul to follow the path back to the throne of the King of Kings. So you must make contact with both aspects of the Word within thyself, and this is provided by God, and unfolded by the true Godman, for Soul to travel along with the Sound step-by-step into the land of pure, eternal bliss.

"Once you have gained contact through ECK with the divine link, the Word of God, Soul is literally pulled out of Its clay temple toward the Heaven of Heavens from which It came, with such force that the world in which you now live is unreal and uninteresting."

The seeker's eyes strained into the dark sky, staring at the brilliant star, at the darkness beyond the star. The star was white, pure and eternal, a bright beacon burning into the night.

He leaned across the river's edge. The haunting Sound beat at him, pulled at him. He seemed no longer to be standing on the earth, but suspended in space. He stretched out his hand across the water—across the hills toward the burning star.

"If you have faith," said the Traveler's voice, "if thy heart is ready, then you can follow the Voice of God back to thy true Home! You can travel back again via the path of ECKANKAR!"

The seeker's mind reeled; the night, the star, and the world reeled around him. He started falling into a deep, dark gulf where the darkness was blacker and deeper. He was falling, reaching out, groping for a hand, grasping at the Guru. The burning star was before him, the roaring Sound in his head, and he knew this was the Voice of God! This was ECKANKAR!

The Great Tree of Life

he seeker was seated in the shade of the great oak tree watching the beauty of the wide, yellow river. His roving glance took in the little town nearby, complete with docks, wide porches, and busy people.

He could sense the old, sweated land of this world, and the color and odors of this land. These were soft tones, as deceptive as the magnificent river moving gracefully between the deep-blue hills, onward toward the sea. Overhead the cool, spring wind whispered through the green leaves of the giant limbs of the oak.

He said half-aloud, "Behold the oak in all its glory. It is like God firmly rooted in the earth, yet reaching upward into the sky."

"Yea, thou art right," replied the Tibetan, stroking his stubbled chin. "Man is but the bird that builds its nest in the oak's branches and seeks shelter from the wind and sun. Nothing is a problem to the oak. It is a law unto itself."

The seeker said, "The oak is like man in that unless it lives in accord with itself, it cannot live in accord with God!"

"Beauty is like the oak," said Rebazar Tarzs. "It is that harmony between joy and pain which begins in the body of man and ends beyond the scope of man's mind.

101

It is but a trial to the body, and a gift to the spirit.

"This is the power which leads man's heart to that of a woman, which is, on this earth, the throne of God. And love is that holy liquor which God has wrung from His great heart and poured into the lover's heart for his beloved. He who can drink this liquor is pure and divine, and his heart has been cleansed of all but pure love! Thus I say that the lover whose heart is drunk with love is drunk with God.

"Live thy life, O my son, live it fully with all its love and pain. Let this be thy understanding in ECKANKAR. Share thy cup with thy beloved, and never fail to help thine own in pain and suffering. This should be thy law unto thyself, my son.

"Thus I say to thee, pity thy brother who can see only with his eyes and no more than the light of the sun which he thinks is lighting the world for his evil. He is blind, although he may have the keenest sight of all. And pity him whose ears can hear nothing more than slander of his neighbors. Even though he can hear the fish swimming in the river channel, he is deaf!

"Pity him whose mouth is made for swallowing rich food to keep the stomach filled; for though he may appreciate fine foods, he is without the true knowledge that bread alone is not enough for man's body.

"And pity him whose tongue can do no more than speak evil of his neighbor, for even though he has true oratory, or a silver tongue for speech, he is without God's own goodness.

"At last, pity him whose hands are used for injury of God's own creatures; for though his hands may be gentle, he is not good at heart and cannot have God's mercy until he learns that all creation is God's creation.

"All life is naked, my son. So you must watch and keep thyself covered with purity, the true symbolic robe of God, which gives thee humbleness before all creations, and before thine own Lord Almighty, the SUGMAD. Therefore, if pain is the hidden purifier of keeping thyself clean, then have no fear of God for He is taking away that which is evil within thyself.

"Be like the great oak under whose branches you sit. Raise thy head and heart to God, but keep thy roots firmly clinging to the earth; and drink from this land, and make death and happiness thy companions. Love God, and give Him that which is from the purity of heart, made clean by suffering. Increase thy longing for Him and exalt Him with holy desire — and make no action within thy life unless you first ask God.

"Man's final glory is like the top of a tree, which has ascended into the heavens from its roots, into the divine sky, above all its fellow trees, and gone beyond duality of the earth into the unity of true space, of light and air.

"Truth is the only source of knowledge, and man is the mirror for Truth. Yet man cannot receive more than what Soul can hold. Man reflects that which is within himself, and you must be the clear mirror to reflect Truth!"

The Traveler stopped talking and closed his eyes and appeared to sleep.

The seeker contemplated upon what the Tibetan had said. The sweet shade of the oak swung behind Rebazar Tarzs, and a light gleamed upon the brown flesh of his bare feet.

Purity

hat is purity, Sire?" asked the seeker, watching an old crane fishing along the sleepy, willowed point of the island where sluggish eddies whirled past.

"Purity is the truth of Soul dwelling in God, my son," replied Rebazar, walking up to the side of the seeker. "When man purifies his consciousness, then he begins to walk the path of God in a straightforward manner via the path of ECK. If you seek the things of this world, then you will be in darkness, although you may have plenty of material things.

"But what does it profit a man to gain possession of the whole world and lose his own Soul?"

The seeker shook his head. "I do not know the mysteries of the beyond, O Sire. Please teach me!"

The Tibetan smiled and spoke on. "Time after time God sends His supreme son into the world to revive the often-forgotten Prada-Vidya, (meaning the God-knowledge) and emphasizing its importance to man.

"But man forgets God. He does not realize that it is a matter of common knowledge and experience that light comes from light and life from life. God is both Light and life. He is the source of both, and all living creatures live in Him and their light comes from Him.

"So I tell you that if you seek the Light in this world, then this world will become light for thee, and all the darkness of the earth and its illusions will vanish. Then God's Voice will speak to thee, each word filled with divine wisdom and understanding, and you will transcend all things in this world.

"God can only give the Light to those who are pure in heart. Until you drop the barrier of thy ego, the Light will not reach thee. No message can be given thee, and it is a waste of effort for the teacher to attempt it. Truth is but a spear, and those who are not ready for the truth of God will wound themselves upon its point.

"Therefore I say unto you that if you are not purified, then you are not true to thyself, and unable to give the truth to others. Therefore, any man who desires to give the truth or do the work of God must first be faithful and true to that divine self within him.

"Purity calls for the highest within man. You cannot slander nor can you see the evil in others. If you look for the good in those around thee, then you will bring out the good within them, and make thy neighbor manifest his good qualities. Dwell upon the good within thy neighbor and thus you will exalt the good in him, and bring out the good in thyself. Thy good qualities will not come forth unless you see them in the world about you.

"Do not listen to one who preaches or acts with evil, lest you should bring about thy own undoing, for the fault lies within thyself for listening to that teacher. Open thyself to receive evil and in doing so become one with him who preaches evil. Yea, I tell you that it is true there are rogues even among the spiritual orders, but it is thy fault if you will find favor with them. Use thy discrimination and mingle only with the good. Then you purify thyself!

"So, do not desire that for others which you do not desire for thyself, for then you bring to thyself that which is not a part of Soul, and you will not be giving anything that is a part of thyself. Take the shortcut to God and give of thyself to all.

"To be pure, then, become humble and meek before thy God, and thy neighbor. Raise the good qualities in all thy fellow creatures and you will become exalted, for God gives only to those who live for their fellowman.

"To become pure you must do three things: first, chant the holy names of God constantly upon thy lips; secondly, do everything in the name of the SUGMAD, thy Father; and third, love the SUGMAD with all thy passion, and also thy neighbor. These three spiritual practices will make thee pure, my son.

"If you know these spiritual truths and fail to practice them, it is like one who has lighted his lantern and closed his eyes to the light. So I tell you that you are the light, and are to learn the spiritual truths. But leave them not in thy mind to be practiced, but manifest and act upon the spiritual truths as I teach you here, for it does you little good to think spiritual truths unless you put them into spiritual action. These spiritual truths will make thee pure and transform thy life if you will do as I say.

"So listen to me. The pure Light of the spiritual consciousness is the true Light of God. This is the Light which is given man by God. The Godmen, the true sons of the supreme Lord, are the fortunate who can dwell in that Light at all times. The communion between God and His true sons is continuous. You see?"

The Tibetan took a seat under the oak and closed his eyes. The seeker watched the crane fishing off the point of the island and pondered the words of his teacher.

The Sermon
in the Market Square

ebazar Tarzs strolled majestically through the marketplace of Srinagar, followed by the seeker. The early morning light was still a misty gray, rising over the Kashmir hills beyond the river. The tall, sari-clad women had filled their scrubbed stalls with homegrown flowers, rice, and garden products.

The taciturn men stood by the stalls watching the Tibetan with dark admiring eyes. And as he passed a knot of silent watchers, one disentangled himself and stopped the Godman.

"If you are a great Soul," he said, "give us the Truth of God."

The Master smiled happily. "Ah, the truth of God. So ye would like to know the truth? The real truth? But who can explain the glories of God with words?"

The man spoke defensively. "We have suffered much, great one. Nobody has come here before to teach us. Truth, they say, lies beyond the verbal expression of man. If you can even communicate partial insights we will come to know thy purpose, and would be led into the stage where we may achieve fuller realization."

"That is true," said Rebazar, spreading his hands. "But truth has always existed and is unborn and indestructible. It is not of any nature except as the will of

113

God, and does not belong to the categories of things which exist or do not exist. Neither does it have form or appearance.

"Therefore, I say, there are three working factors in the philosophy of God's Truth. First, the prime mover and life-giver is the Spirit or Word, or Sound Current; second is mind; and the third, matter, of which the body and senses, as the instruments of action, are made.

"Thus, the entire creation below the second grand division is composed of two parts: namely, Spirit, which is all good and pure; and matter, which is always the negative part of Spirit.

"My friends, ye must know that ye are but a drop from the ocean of God's mercy and love, and this, I say, is the Supreme Being, ITSELF. Ye, as the drop of pure Spirit, art so mixed with matter that ye come in bondage and must be released from it. Unless aided by a Supreme Son ye are always liable to yield to temptation and will deteriorate and will sink down into matter.

"Matter is necessary for Spirit life in the lower kingdom. But for matter, God would be one huge ocean filling all space. Before creation, all Spirits lay at the feet of the Lord in an unmanifested mass. These Spirits could have no separate form, no individuality, nor individual existence except by a mixture of matter. Thus they could attain no knowledge of their true self in God. As fire is necessary to light any ignitable substance, so is Spirit required to give life to matter. At the death of every creature the liberated Spirit merely changes Its matter cover, or in other words, takes up Its abode in a life form of some other creature.

"Therefore, I tell ye that a devotee, when merged into the Spirit Current of the supreme Being, is like this liberated Spirit, and can assume his individuality in any form so desired, at his own pleasure.

"Soul is like a cup which has been turned upside down and cannot receive the waters of heaven. The Spiritual Traveler appears and turns the cup face upward so it can be filled, and Soul is drenched with the spiritual Sound Current and becomes holy.

"The divine Sound Current is composed of five known strains of melodies, and is the connecting link between the created Soul and the Creator. It is the ladder by which Soul travels upward on Its journey into the highest Kingdom of Heaven.

"If ye seekers desire to become God, ye need not study anything of this worldly nature. Study only how to avoid seeking for or clinging to anything. If ye seek nothing but God, then ye will have no need of anything but God, for He will give all ye need in this life.

"And when ye pass from this earth into the Heavenly Kingdom, God will have His angels there to take care of thee and to help ye be free of all that excess baggage which ye have brought with thee.

"So I plead of thee, good friends, look for God within thyselves, and pray that He will fill thy cups until they overflow!"

The Tibetan turned away from them and walked on, while the seeker followed, noticing the brightness of the marketplace. He wondered at what made the Light shine within the building, and from whence It came, since the sun had not yet risen.

Freedom

he seeker stood in the field, by the river, looking at the girl long and tenderly, and the bright sunlight filled the world in yellow and green.

Her laughter was bright on the air, spinning its echoes on a gay breeze, and her eyes were gentle, now distant, now soft and tender. He felt, inside with Soul and outside, the touch of her hands upon his shoulders.

The world spun and danced upside down and widened into the horizon where the white clouds hung low. He saw nothing but the eyes of the woman and love shining upon her brow.

The Master's voice spoke to them. Turning, they saw him standing calmly among the high grasses. "If ye seek love, you will find it truly in the heart of a woman," he said. "Yea, but it is not within the kisses that you find her greatest love, but within her heart. Her kiss is only the symbol of that which God sends through her heart. For indeed woman is the greatest instrument of God.

"So I tell you to seek only the highest in thy beloved. And in finding her true love, then you will find freedom, and in finding this great attribute you find humility. For the greatest freedom of Soul is in humility.

"If you love thy woman for masculine conquest, then you will have neither love nor freedom from attachment. Then you have lost all joy and believe more in the things which do not exist, and there is no freedom for thee, for you are always seeking, unknowingly to the senses, the ways to break the chains of attachment.

"It is never a true love unless the lover possesses at least two divine qualities—gratitude and purity—and if he does not have these, then he will only succeed in bringing woe unto himself.

"The degree and nature of a man's love for God, through a woman, extends to the highest altitudes of Spirit. If he fails to understand her nature, that which is beyond this world, then he has failed in his search for God; for the woman, if she knows her nature, can lead man to God. This is her duty and responsibility in this world.

"Freedom and independence of body, mind, and Soul are the qualities which a woman should take upon herself to help her beloved to develop. Love and purity are the two qualities that man should see that develop in woman. If these qualities are developed in both, and respected in one another, they will rise above this world, together, into the Kingdom of Heaven.

120

"Love for woman should give man a greater love for God; and in developing a greater love for God, man's ego will dissolve and its limited, petty self will be overcome and he will find transcendentalism of the Lord.

"So I tell ye both to look to the sunrise each day, for everything in the past must be forgotten and each day must be a new start upon the path of God. Remember that Lot's wife was warned not to look back into her past, and it is well known that Lot, himself, was partly responsible for her transgression and also suffered. Keep thy vision fixed upon the future in eternity, and forget the errors of the past.

"Nothing can be taught thee, my friends, which is not already concealed as potential knowledge in the unfolding of thy Souls. All perfection of the outer self is but the realization of the eternal perfection of Spirit within thyselves.

"In order for the lover to become the man of God, which is his ultimate goal, so the woman must encourage and help him in forgetting what he always thinks he wants to be. In order for him to find himself he must go out of himself, and in order to live he must die. And so this applies also to woman!

"Love is like a slow, consuming fire which starts in the center of man's heart and slowly moves outward, destroying all that is in its path. Nothing can stop love, and even when it appears to be quenched, it will break out somewhere else. So it is with freedom.

"Love comes first in the heart, and with the development of love then ye get freedom; and then with freedom one gets all truth. For after all, truth contains all things, yet man in his state in this world can develop singularly. Therefore, it is best to start with the virtue of love.

"If God wants ye for anything, there is nothing ye can do about it. He will draw ye unto Him in some manner or other without ye ever realizing it. Through the heart of a woman, or a child, it matters not to Him.

"I tell ye this, that nothing else matters. Love one another, but love that which is thy God within thee, and then ye will find lasting love."

With that the Sat Guru turned and walked through the field toward the river, with the seeker and the girl watching him. Their faces were lighted with a divine glow.

The Trembling
of a Star

he seeker and the girl sat under a tree by the river, looking at the millions of stars flung across the heavens like bright jewels. The girl's face shone wondrously in the starlight. The perfume of a field of nearby spring flowers wafted by on the soft breeze which rippled the waters that lapped the sandy bank.

The girl whispered softly, "Look. Look at the star!" He lifted his head and looked to see the marvelous star shining brightly through the top of the willows. He thought that was the star which belonged to them, but he could not speak for her lips held more promise than his words.

Turning, he spoke to Rebazar Tarzs. "Sire, what of the star?" he asked, loosing his hands from the girl's shoulders. "What of the bright one trembling in the heavens above the hills?"

"The star of God," replied the Tibetan, gazing at both with eyes shining brightly in the darkness. "That particular star is sacred to the legend of Easter, whose day will dawn within a few hours. It was the star that gleamed so brightly when the Lord Jesus was resurrected that wondrous morning centuries ago. It was a herald to the world that death had been overcome. Just as the star of Bethlehem was the signal to all people that a savior had been born, God hung another star in His sky for the resurrection of the son whom man crucified.

"I tell ye that the very stars in the morning sky tremble in heavenly bliss in memory of that glorious day when Jesus showed the world that death could be overcome.

"Yet man does not know these things. We do not feed truth to the unbeliever, for when it is done man will injure him who gives the word of God. Each of us has a duty in this world to God, and those who are able to carry a little part of it, great or small, are indeed blessed.

"So ye see, man's greatest fight is against his fault of not trying to avoid or overcome ignorance, or the darkness of the world. To overcome it requires wisdom, and the best way to acquire wisdom is by unremitting endeavor. Ye do not get it any other way than by contemplation.

"The bright star that trembles this morning in the heavens is an ancient symbol of the whole cosmic universe. For when the Lord sent a divine son into this world, He did so to prove that man can overcome death also, as Jesus did; and when the divine son goes through the process of death as we all do daily by practicing ECK, the whole universe goes through the process of regeneration. Whatever a great Soul like Jesus does upon this earth affects mankind throughout the whole life of the earth.

"The star represents a divine channel through which the Lord diffuses the rays of love upon the world, and those holy vibrations touch all God's creatures and awaken them to their destiny again, which, of course, is the great cosmic plan for man's desire to be aroused to discover his true destiny in eternity.

"Therefore, I say that every Supreme Son who comes to this plane does so by his own free choice to help his fellowman. He need not assume the mortal garb and suffer, for indeed it would be his privilege to sit at the feet of God throughout all eternity. However, such could serve their purpose in this world, for greater experiences in the service of God, and without thought of reward, and yet their reward is beyond any conception of man's mind.

"What is a man of God, ye ask?"

"I tell ye that a man of God is he who is not affected by the changes which may come around him. He is the same, be the weather stormy or hot, dark or light; and he retains his sense of balance and values no matter what happens. So I tell ye that as long as there is a necessity in thy life for birth, there will be a necessity for resurrection.

"When Souls evolve to this point, they are free from the Wheel of Life and no longer need to incarnate upon this earth, and the necessity for either birth or death is done away with. So the greatest knowledge is that of God Consciousness; by becoming one with ECK, ye are released from the Wheel of Life.

"The star of God trembles this night because the both of ye are reborn into the Kingdom of Heaven. Ye have found thyselves in the far-flung worlds of the cosmic kingdom.

"If ye walk the middle path of understanding, ye will arrive at the end of the worldly wheel of birth and death, and be like the star that trembles in the sky of this early morning, or the river that flows between the hills and down through the valley to empty into the sea!"

The seeker looked again at the trembling star and wondered. He felt the girl's hand clasp his and felt her against his shoulder. He was thinking that this was the world of his life and nothing else mattered but the three of them — yet soon the Traveler would send him out into the world to fulfill his mission.

No Greater Love

t was hot among the broad rows of white crosses in the little graveyard above the city, and the seeker could smell the blossoms of the plum trees clustered around a little church on the knoll. He watched the Master strolling among the rows of graves, studying the inscriptions on the headstones.

April in the old graveyard always brought sharp burdens of sadness and melancholy, with its beauty merging into the reality of memories to the seeker. He looked at the waters of the river glistening in the sun like tiny glints of mirrored gold. To the far side of the horizon of snowy peaks was a mass of colors with a gay carnival-like impression, and partly hidden in the blue haze.

He walked up to the Master's side, and saw that the great Soul was studying a headstone that had the inscription, "No Greater Love Hath Man Than To Lay Down His Life For Another." The seeker explained that it was the grave of a low-caste Indian who had given his life to save a drowning white child in the river.

The Tibetan said, "It is true that when man gives his life for another, he will be saved. That Soul touched the unseen power which we call the sea of life. By doing so he gained God's mercy and grace for himself!"

131

"It is strange to me that the beauty of life cannot be measured by mere attitudes and opinions," said the seeker, listening to the crickets chirping among the weeds. "Because love is the greatest of all things, man is ever seeking it."

"Love is God," replied Rebazar Tarzs. "When you wish to bathe in the river, you go to the edge where the water is shallow and say that you have bathed in the river. Thus to love and receive the real benefit of God's love, we must give up that finite self within us and do deeds for the sake of our fellowman. That is the reason why this Soul is honored by his fellowman and enjoys bliss in heaven with God. He gave without hesitation.

"Love is the essence, spirit, soul, and life of all that exists or appears to exist, itself unchangeable and immortal.

"Love is most sublime, having its origin in the House of God. In whatever heart love blooms, that Soul will be lifted and carried to the highest abode of the Supreme SUGMAD. All good virtues and goodness itself will gradually find their true home in the heart in which love dwells, and all other qualities will wither and die.

"So I tell you that where pure love dwells there

forms a link with Spirit, or the love current, from Its source—the Divine Fountainhead.

"If you have sincere love for God you will be attracted toward this by grace, mercy, and the holy Light which will gradually illumine thy own self, and then all outward desires will gradually disappear.

"Love, I say, has no bonds, knows no restrictions, and is not limited by conditions; and like its source, God, is omnipresent, omnipotent, and omniscient in all its beneficial results.

"Every wave of love rising in the lover's heart brings tidings of good news and joy from his beloved, and every thought springing up in such a heart is a signal of good works and services for the sake of his beloved.

"God loves and takes special care of those who love Him with all their heart and Soul, and gradually draws them toward Himself, the center of pure Light. Love is holy and pure in its essence, and man must keep himself forever dwelling in this Light.

"If you conquer maya, or illusion, then you will become the master of thy life and death and will be a light unto this world to all, a liberator to those who are seeking, and there will be no longer any distinction between God and thyself in the inner kingdom.

"To approach the source of love, ye must first approach and catch its Spirit Current and follow Its course back to the Godhead. The highway to God lies within thine own body.

"True philosophy is that which leads the seeker to the region of sublime love and teaches the way of traveling the regions where false truths and comparative truths prevail, and reaching the most sublime house of God.

"So I tell you that the attainment of the knowledge and actuality of love in the highest sphere of heaven is called true and perfect salvation."

The Sat Guru strolled away from the grave down through the rows of crosses toward the little church, while the seeker followed, wondering at the words which thundered within himself.

Death

he seeker stood on the edge of the riverbank, watching the sun peek its golden head over the far Himalayan peaks and shoot long shafts of light across the broad waters flowing toward the sea.

A strange feeling arose within him as if he were being resurrected from death and stood on the very brink of an unknown world which was yet for him to explore. He was coming out of darkness into the light.

Turning, he said to the Tibetan, "I, Soul, reach out into the darkness, O sire, seeking ever thyself in the light of the rising sun, but find thee not."

"It is like death which has covered thy body and you look again for the light and find it upon looking," Rebazar Tarzs replied. "Death is only a passing of Soul through the veil of maya into a brighter light. You will find death, so to speak, on all planes."

The seeker said passionately, "Sire, take me as your own and temper me. Make me like the fine steel of the shoe of a golden mare. Give me the splendor of thy blessings, mercies, and knowledge."

"I will speak to thee of death," said the Tibetan. "I will give thee the truth of God, so you may understand and know. Let me enlighten thee.

"True philosophy is that which leads the sincere seeker to the region of truth. So I will give thee truth and put thy feet upon the path of ECK to God. Knowledge without love for God is futile and tends toward darkness. Love turns everything to God, and even overcomes death.

"So I tell you that it is known that death of thy clay temple is only the beginning of life for thee to really know God. If you practice what I tell you, then you shall have no more fear of death, and all that is becomes holy. You find the only true joy is to escape from thine own limited little self. Until you love God with all thine heart and Soul, this world will be filled with contradictions.

"Fill thyself with Light, and death cannot overtake thee. Ask God for the Light and Sound to live in peace. Be humble and see that Soul be filled with the simplicity of love. Then thine own true Self, the divine spark, which is truly thee, will alone endure; and the rest of thee will be discarded in order to realize the Real Self which is thine own true Self.

"Listen to my words, O seeker, for I speak naught but truth. You become filled with the Light when you discover God within thyself, and when God opens Himself unto thy senses. As you cannot enter into His Kingdom because you alone do not know the way, then you must depend upon the mercy of the Blessed One,

138

for He sends His son to show thee the path of ECK to return homeward.

"If you know that death is only an illusion, then there is little need for thee to have cause for fear. Truth sustains you, and this clay temple is dissolved when the physical body wears out; but the Soul which owes Its origin, life, and growth to God, will remain forever in the highest mansion of the Lord.

"The first and original perfect form created by the Spiritual Current is that which man seeks for perfection. But this perfect form is within thyself; you need not have death to see It and learn of It. It is a work of God's creation, can never die, and always shines Its light before the world.

"God is a boundless ocean of Spirit and love, and man being a drop from this ocean, it follows that he can never die and will always be as the fish in the river, forever swimming in the ocean of God's mercy and love.

"So I tell you that pure and holy love is always ready to give whatever it has for the sake of its love, and the benefit of its fellow creatures, without the thought of reward. So if man is full of purity, he thinks and lives in God's wisdom. He needs little else in his life.

"So in order to gain life you must first die, and by dying in this physical body you will find the divine life.

If you cannot die once, in this clay temple, then you cannot die daily as Saint Paul says in the Bible. And by dying daily you are able to become one with God, to be thy true Self; for the secret of thy identity is hidden in the love and grace of thy true Father, our Lord God, ruler of all the universes in creation.

"So in ending this little discussion with thee, I will tell thee that every lover of God will gladly give up his body, one time, yea a million times—as it matters not to him how many times he is reincarnated. Thus he is more aware that being understood holds more contradictions than being misunderstood. This is because he knows that those who understand will face themselves in the inner world with confidence."

The Master folded his hands behind his back and started pacing the bank of the river in long, graceful strides, while the seeker watched silently. He was filled with a mysterious Light and Sound.

Practice of the Zikar

ire," said the seeker as they walked through the old wharf, where small boats were loading cargo for upriver trips into the foothills of the Himalayas. "Thou art always speaking of the Zikar. What is Zikar? Wilt thou please enlighten me?"

"Yea," replied the Tibetan, stopping to look at huge stocks of food stacked row upon row against the walls. "Zikar is the art of making contact with the Audible Life Stream within thyself by the inward chanting of your secret word. Of course, this is all in accordance with the teachings of the true Godman!

"Conscious understanding is the privilege of man, and it becomes a privilege when earned through the seeking of God, for God's own sake, via the Spiritual Exercises of ECK. This is the chief result from using the Zikar.

"The path of God through ECK is a practical one and cannot be learned from books or those versed in books. It can be learned only from a living Godman, who will give thee the art of avoiding the difficulties which you will meet on the inner path. He gives the actual inner experience of Light and Sound to all who sit for the spiritual exercises.

"This experience has to be developed by daily practice, by the fixing of hours. The attention is to be fixed upon a spot between the eyes, technically the Tisra Til, or the Third Eye.

"If you consciously strive to become the Godman, then you will lose God. By intention to bring thyself into harmony with the Light you will instantly be taken from It. Did Jesus not say that whosoever tried to save his life would lose it?

"All understanding must come when you are totally aware to the limits of thy mental and physical potentialities. Once liberated from the body through the ECK, you will see it as a husk clothed in rags and find thyself, Soul, inseparable from the Eternal Spirit.

"You must sit in silence chanting the sacred names of the SUGMAD. The practice is a weapon against all dangers. It is a password to all spiritual planes, gives strength and sustenance to the body and mind during trouble and affliction, brings Soul nearer to God, and achieves happiness while on this plane.

"Equal attention must be paid to the Light and Sound. Usually the Light appears first and then the Sound, and then the radiant form of the Master will appear of itself. When he does appear, you have to absorb your attention into him.

"The Sound is developed through the different planes. Each plane has a distinct Sound of its own, though all of them emanate from the same source — the difference being caused by the varying degrees of density resulting from difference in the proportion of matter and Spirit in each plane.

"This I tell you, if you seek within to find God and have found Him, then thy own ideals are fulfilled. It depends upon thee, for every man is the way and truth unto himself. Speaking to his disciples, Jesus said, 'I am the way, the truth, and the life,' but he was speaking from the Christ consciousness and not as Jesus the man.

"So I speak to thee from the God plane, and not as a man. The divine source of love can be thy own for the taking. You need only thy own self for the way, and the Godman to give thee encouragement and a lift along the path into heaven.

"God is that active, moving force. IT has in ITSELF the Spirit, and briefly dwelling upon the term Spirit, it is said not to be so mysterious as it might sound. Spirit is that aspect of God, the very being of the divine self, which makes up the worlds of reality. Spirit is often the word used for the divine power, but in reality the word is a deviation of the Greek term for spiral.

"God is Soul, within my heart, smaller than the tiny creatures or insects that crawl through the grass at our feet. God is the Self within the heart, and greater than the sky, greater than all, within the realm of creation, for He is the creator of all creation.

"So I tell thee, my son, that to approach God, you must do so by the ECK and catch the Light and Sound and follow both back to the source of the truth of all truths. And that highway to reach the spiritual home of God lies within the human body. We must go through the body to Soul in order to reach God, or the Supreme Soul.

"The true source of God is that self which is, and there Soul will live in bliss through all eternity. This is what you must strive for in thy life throughout all the worlds of God."

The seeker watched the divine Soul turn and look curiously at the small boats stacked along the walls, as if he was wondering what they were for, and yet knowing inwardly. The seeker's heart lifted as they walked out of the building into the clear sunlight again.

The True Surrender

rue surrender is the way to God," said Rebazar Tarzs, sitting on the riverbank in the bright morning sunlight. "The ego must give up all so that Soul can transcend Its sheaths in the material world and be liberated for perfect freedom!"

The seeker, watching the Traveler, said, "It is thou who destroys the darkness by the resplendent light of thy knowledge, and this light within me becomes the increasing glory of my own self-revelation."

"Not I, whom you see here in the earthly form," replied Rebazar, smiling broadly, "but the true Master who is not the body but the Divine ECK Power functioning through the body and using it to teach thee and guide thee in the highest possible duty for God's own sake.

"There is a law, if you wish to call it a law, but I say an aspect of God, which reverses itself. The harder man tries to do something with his conscious will, the less he is apt to succeed. Proficiency, and the result of proficiency, comes only to those who have learned the paradoxical art of simultaneously doing and not doing, of combining relaxation with activity, of letting go as a person in order that God may take hold.

"Understanding comes when you are totally aware to the limit of thy mental and physical potentialities. So I tell you if you are consciously striving to become one with God, you are apt to lose everything you have gained. By intention to bring thyself into harmony with the Light you will instantly be taken from it. Did Jesus not say that whosoever tried to save his life would lose it?

"Then I tell you this—to seek the Light consciously is to lose It; to talk of God and the aspects of God is to keep Him from thee; and to seek Him is to have Him always fleeing before thee.

"So you ask then, how does man find God?

"I can tell you this; the way to God is to surrender to God, with thy Self completely and fully, so that nothing else can stand between thee and Him. Surrender is the only way. The surest way to Him is to let God take over Soul; open thyself to Him constantly, to His wisdom and love, and trust to His effect.

"Once you have learned the art of true surrender, Soul is literally withdrawn from Its physical temple to progress to the higher planes from whence It came. Once the inner life is realized, the outer one begins to seem unreal and of little consequence.

"You will reach the true bliss of our Lord when Soul has been polarized with the Eternal Self and consumed by this almighty Soul, when you see constantly the Divine in all things and beings and happenings. Thy heart will be consumed when all thy emotions are summed up in the love for the Divine—of the Divine in ITSELF and for ITSELF; but love too of the Divine in all ITS beings and powers and personalities and forms within the heavens of God.

"When the little self is eradicated through God's pure love, then Soul remains in all Its radiant glory, and then you will be surrendered to Him and will constantly move in accord to His perfect will. Then, only, will you delight in God and the spiritual use of His perfection and fulfillment.

"Ah, but I tell thee, perfect self-consecration is the way to perfect self-surrender to the beloved Master Soul of all the many spheres of Heaven.

"Beyond life is God. Man must go beyond the transformation of his superficial, narrow and human way of thinking, seeing, feeling, and being into the deep and wide spiritual consciousness, and the integrated Godself in that true realm which is called the Kingdom of Heaven.

151

"The source of eternal bliss is the God-self in all. Only because of the infinite love and mercy of God can man learn to realize the lessons which he must undergo on earth; and that inherent in him is the source of infinite bliss, and that most of man's suffering is his struggle to uncover the divine Self within.

"True happiness can be found only in the Eternal Home where Soul must someday return; and as long as thy own true self looks to anything but God, It will not travel toward the Kingdom of God, but remain here on earth in chains.

"What do you wish to do? Live in freedom with God, or spend thy time in this earth prison?"

With that the Tibetan concluded and sat watching his disciple with a strange smile. The seeker laughed softly and shook his head, knowing the divine Soul at his side knew everything in his heart.

Grasping God

ou are trying to hold God in your hands," said the Traveler seated under the broad branches of the great oak in the lotus posture. "You can never grasp God to the extent that He is fully thine own. You find the great Reality is elusive, unable to catch up in thy hands, and hardly real to thine inner senses. Is this not true?"

The seeker said curiously, "Yes, Sire. This is true. It seems that the more I seek God, the less I have of Him. Why is this?"

"The answer to thy question is a paradox to the mind, my son," Rebazar replied softly, brushing his hair with a brown hand. "It is because the inner order of thy life is that of God. To get in mystical union with thy own creator is through illumination, the Sound Current, and thy Master. All the basis of life is unchanging, unruffled, and not stirred by anything which reflects from the outside, or the external.

"I tell you this: God is not reflected in the images of what surrounds you here, but the real is what existed before all this universe began to exist, and before you came into thine own body, and long after you leave it. You see?

"The universal body of God is reality, and all the worldly forms are phenomenal and shaped as they are needed in their respective places to fulfill the destiny of the divine purpose in the cosmic plan.

"When you seek God, thine own senses will rebel, for since the senses have been the object of thine own self for many generations, the pattern of life which you have built up causes an entity to exist within thee, and this little self grows upon thy objective senses. Its only goal in life is to satisfy itself and see that it exists; nothing else matters—and it cares little about the physical self, hardly more than the true Soul cares about the body. Therefore, it struggles to maintain its rulership of the body of man—even into the three worlds beyond.

"So when you seek God for God's sake, then you must remember that this self must be completely banished.

"Many of the Christian saints write of their struggles against this force, to overcome it and reach God; yet I tell you that the struggle is not necessary. There is an easier path to God.

"The way to God is difficult to those who struggle against the little self and look to the obstacles in the path. The difference between heaven and earth is not hardly a hairbreadth's in difference.

"I will illustrate it by telling you of a great Saint who struggled for God, intensely in silence, holding to the robe of the divine Soul with grasping fingers and begging to maintain his grasp. When awakened, he discovered that his hands were grasping his own robes. You see?

"So I tell you this. Should you want God to stand before thee in full clarity, the way is this. Never to be for, nor against anything—for this is the mind's greatest struggle. It is God's nature to be always in the balance, never too much and never too little.

"All maya must be driven from the mind, and you must see that God is! Seek IT for ITS own sweet sake, and by stopping all movement to become rested in His beloved arms; then you will be rested within thine own sweet self, and all movements will have ceased.

"You must polarize Soul with that of the Master Soul, and then calm and peacefulness will overcome thee, and the struggle to God is lost in the beauty of thy Lord's own presence. As you sink deeper into God, then find IT, all thy frantic struggles to grasp the hem of ITS robe will have disappeared and you have IT quietly in thine own hands—rather, IT will have thee quietly in ITS hands!

"Did you ever see the babe struggle in its mother's arms because something disturbed its little heart? And all the soothing love that the mother could give was lost because the struggle was greater than its understanding? But then comes the moment when her love penetrates the little one's outer self and enters into the babe's heart, and lo, its struggles cease. Then it allows the mother's tender, gentle love to pervade.

"So I tell you that to embrace God is to give up thy false views and look upon all with the eyes of love. Do not take sides, and forget thy clinging to, and trust only in the path which the Master has set thy own feet upon. To pursue the Light and Sound is to lose them; so then you must do everything with effortless effort and let that which is the true Self within thee do all. Be relaxed in thy seeking—with confidence!

"God is none other than the all, and the all is none other than God. So you must obey and surrender thyself sweetly to God, and let IT be the all in thy heart."

With this the Master ceased and rose to his feet, motioning to the seeker. As they walked away from the river's banks toward the little town, Rebazar picked up a market basket and swung it casually in his brown hand.

Sermon to the Fishes

ebazar Tarzs stood on the edge of the sandy riverbank, a majestic figure looking down at the clear water where hundreds of fishes were lined in wavering schools with eyes upturned to him.

His hand reached into the market basket and took fried rice to scatter upon the crystal surface, but the little fishes let the crumbs sink slowly through to the sandy bottom of the riverbed.

"See?" said the Traveler in his wonderful voice. "The little creatures of the water are more interested in the spiritual food than bread for the body. Is it not true then that they know the Voice of God?"

The seeker said curiously, "I would grant that, Sire. Thy word touches all hearts, be it the tiniest creature or those in the lofty heights of the Eternal Home where thy sublime creations dwell. Thy words spontaneously instill in all the feeling of love for all fellow beings. And this feeling will supersede the tendency of separateness, and rule over the hearts of all. Then all happiness reigns."

"Yea, that is right," replied Rebazar, turning his attention to the shadowy figures of the fishes in the water. "Little brothers and sisters, I tell you to love one another. And above all to love God, and then to love thy neighbors.

"To love God is the right way to love thy fellow creatures. If ye have love for others in the same way as ye feel for thy own dear ones, ye love God.

"If instead of robbing one another ye help thyselves in hunger, then ye are loving God.

"If ye suffer in the sufferings of thy fellow creatures and feel the happiness which others have, then ye are loving God and thy fellow creatures.

"Now that ye are the fishes of the water, ye must endure thy lot with patience and contentment, accepting it as the will of thy creator, for this is loving God.

"Ye must know and understand and feel that the greatest act of devotion and worship of God is not to hurt or harm any of His fellow creatures, and if ye practice this then ye are loving God.

"Ye must know that there is nothing in all His creation but to love God as IT ought to be loved, and must live for God and die for God. Ye must know that the goal of all life is nothing more than to love God and find IT as thy own Self.

"Happiness in the midst of all adversity can be felt only by touching the very core of Soul, and then ye will have God in thy life, and then ye are loving God.

"If man, in his vain ignorance, deceives thee by giving thee food on a hook and ye are caught, eaten, and digested by man, then know that ye are not dead, for that self which is within thee cannot die, and this is loving God.

"Be ye guided by Love and Truth. This is the simple way that leads to God. By establishing thy own love in one another, which is the unchangeable truth, then ye can hope to be established in abiding peace, and this is loving God.

"If ye know that God is everlastingly working in silence, unobserved and unheard except by those who experience His infinite silence, then ye will know that thy place as the fishes of the river is justified in the harmony of all His creation. And by knowing this, then ye are loving God.

"Be ye understanding of the truth that ye are examples of goodness to one another, and the example of God's creation to all His creatures of the world. Understand this and ye are loving God.

"Be happy that ye can serve God in thy own form, little fishes, for God in all ITS grace and mercy has granted ye life in thy own manifested shape in order to climb the scale to His heights. Ye are on the divine journey to reach thy true Home in the Kingdom of Heaven.

By knowing this sublime truth ye are loving God.

"Know ye then that time has no place in the world of God, and that it matters little to IT if the creatures of His creations are little fishes or man. For as long as ITS creations love IT, they are advancing toward becoming one with the Spirit of God. By thy understanding of this, ye are loving God.

"What I have told ye, little brothers, is from the heart of God, and there must be no faltering of thy love and understanding for thy own selves, for God loves thee greatly. Ye are the brotherhood of the water world, based on the realized Oneness of God.

"God has granted us all His divine love and mercy and blessings. May the blessings be!"

A larger fish raised its head above the water and in silence worked its jaws, and the Tibetan bowed deeply, then took a bowl of rice from the basket and poured the contents upon the water.

The seeker watched in amazement as the fish turned from the bank and began feeding upon the rice.

The Master's Gaze

he seeker was watching the sunlight upon the far blue mountains, and his thoughts were upon the Traveler. He had heard many times about the Master's gaze, but not having experienced it, rather doubted just what it might be.

Then he turned, letting his gaze sweep across the river, saw the wild geese on the sandbar, and the broad, yellow river flowing onward to the sea; then it came to rest upon the Master approaching from out of the willows along the banks.

Looking up he saw the Tibetan's gaze upon him and all qualms which had been in his heart swept away. There was a torrent of love pouring out of Rebazar's eyes, like a great electrical current. It swept over him, binding him in its spell, and the great bearded face became a shining countenance. Those eyes were deep dark pools of loving fire.

It struck him so strongly he could not stand the Master's gaze. It tore away all finiteness within him. He looked away, wondering what had come over him — knowing a feeling unworthy of the Master's gaze.

"If you look into the mirror thy eyes meet with the true image," said the Tibetan in his softest voice. "If you look into the eyes of God then you see also the true image of thyself as Soul. If you feel unworthy, it is

167

because you do not know thine own true self. To know thyself is great, but to have understanding of thine own self is greater than knowledge.

"It is true that wisdom begets wisdom, but it is also known in the spiritual realms of God that love begets all. Have love and ye have all, even God. And pray tell me what more does man want than the love for God? Even though you love without expectations of reward, you will get the Love of God, if you love God greatly.

"The Law of Love is of a paradoxical nature in the seven spheres of heaven, for it is the only true quality of God, and the only quality which is of its own nature.

"Let me tell you this. Mind is of a dual nature, for it can change from the good to the negative, from the negative to the good, within the minute fraction of a second. Love is permanent — the all-existent, all-knowing, and all-present. This is the great, majestic power of God which sweeps down from heaven into the lower realms to help mankind in its struggle to reach the true, eternal Home.

"The warm, all-embracing love which God pours upon His creations is not always the beautiful and magnificent, but many times a terrifying sight to that devotee whose eyes are first open to the cosmic worlds.

Yet this is the play of maya which clouds and confuses the senses to cause fear within the heart of man.

"Love holds the key to all problems. It has been possible through divine love for man to become as God, and when God becomes man it is also due to His love for man.

"I will tell you this. Love is dynamic in action and contagious in effect. Pure love, then, is matchless in majesty and has no parallel in power; and there is no darkness where it exists, and no darkness which can stand its power. I say that it is the undying flame which sets life aglow, and the lasting emancipation of man depends upon his love for God and upon God's love for all the creatures of His worlds.

"So when you see the love pouring from the eyes of the Master upon his devotee, then you must know that all is love, and where there is love there is oneness, and in complete oneness, that God is realized completely at all times and upon every cosmic plane in creation.

"So the Master pours his love upon the devotee to lift that Soul higher upon the path of God. It is as Jesus said, that those who came unto him would be lifted up.

"Listen to my word. There is no measure for love, and remember that the spirit of true love is always done in the form of sacrifice; not as you know sacrifice here

169

on this earth, but as deeds done for the Master, or God, in loving kindness, giving up all else to do them.

"To be able to do something for thy beloved is a blessing. Then know that it is thrice blessed to do something for God, for doing something for thy beloved with love is, therefore, doing the deed for God.

"So you will work for the one in many, and then you will find oneness and freedom."

With that the Tibetan turned and walked away in his majestic stride, while the seeker watched. Now he knew what the gaze of the Master was, and the great love current that poured through it. But greater was the impact within him that his life was no longer in his own hands!

The Law of Life

ow I tell you," said Rebazar Tarzs, picking up his sandals, "when you are full of opinions and speculations, God is withdrawn from thee. How can I show thee God unless you first empty thyself of all these worldly things?"

The seeker moved nervously under the giant oak tree, then looked at the Traveler putting on his sandals. "I am seeking that Eternal Presence, O Sire. But it flees away from my hands. Show me how I might grasp It."

"Ah there you show thy inward nature. Instead of striving for something to be added to thy nature, get rid of all unnecessary opinions, prejudices, prides, and the hundred other things that hamper and fetter you. Even thy desire for God is an obstacle. Just go ahead with thy spiritual unfoldment, step-by-step, without thought of good or bad, success or failure. Do not linger where God is, and where God is not, but pass on quickly to where *is* God.

"Where is God? IT is in the nameless region, existing there as the gigantic Ocean of Mercy and Love. Thy own self is the mirror reflecting the solution of thy mind and inner nature. So I tell you not to work for freedom but allow freedom to be the result of work itself.

"So this is the Law of Life, in that nothing is available unless you first obtain wisdom through the treasures stored within thyself. These in turn can be shared abundantly with others, bringing them happiness.

"Man should try to be the master of his own mind and body, to govern his environment peacefully, to lead a pure and selfless life, and to be kind and helpful to all fellow beings. These are man's most important daily tasks while in this world. Therefore, you are the instrument of God, and being the instrument of God, you must conform to the vehicle of teaching, or rather I say the vehicle of the ECK.

"There you must know then that the vehicle is subjected to the instrument, for the latter, as a receiving point of God's vibrations, must then be placed in the proper setting to receive the message of God, from whomever it might be given. This means that the vehicle of the ECK is not confined to hermitages in remote mountains, or deserts, for it transcends all customs, all sects, all life, all places, and all time, and is as apt to be found in the city as in the country.

"Therefore, I say again, that the vehicle of ECK might not be a guru, teacher, master, or even a person. It can be something beyond all these. It can be thy own self, or the Voice of God, and mayhaps even Nature herself who teaches thee.

"Truth is perfect and complete within itself. It is nothing newly discovered, for it has always existed. So I say that Truth is never far away from thee. It is always near. Again I say, do not run to it, nor even walk to it, because many times the fact exists that every step you take toward Truth will lead you from it.

"Let the thoughts of other people, and I include thy own teacher's precepts, fail to move thee, and do not follow their thoughts. Instead, learn to listen to the Voice within thy own self. In time you will learn that your body and mind will blend in unity, and you will realize the oneness with all life. And here I take time to point out to thee that even a delicate movement of thy own dualistic thoughts will hold you away from entering the gates of Heaven.

"Those who talk too much about the Supreme ECK and those who talk too much about realization are usually wandering around in their own minds, and are in the throes of struggle. If you will stop and think upon this fact, that the ability to contemplate does not come easily, then you will know that too many hope to find it as the easy path to God.

"Many of the saints have been in silence for years before they became adept in the art of ECK and the ability to leave their body at will. It is said that Saint Paul had to study the art of inner silence for eight years in the Arabian Desert before he was able to say that he 'died daily.' So I tell you that if you desire to become a saint, you will never be one.

"The Law of Life, or in a simpler term the Law of Realization, is that certain principle within each man which reverses itself when man makes an effort to know God. You seek God in a manner, which is not seeking IT. You seek IT by opening thy own inner self to IT and letting IT direct thy life as IT desires. It is an inner awareness that you gain through a certain relenting grace and understanding.

"So I tell you that if you try to see God through ITS forms, or if you try to hear IT through ITS voices, you will never reach IT and will remain forever a stranger to ITS divine grace."

The seeker stared at the Tibetan, who rose and went over to the riverbank to study a wet, green bullfrog sitting on a half-submerged limb. The frog croaked hoarsely, then sailed into the water with a sharp plop. Rebazar smiled broadly.

The Divine Journey

"The divine journey begins now," said the Tibetan, bathing in the shallows of the sandbar while the golden sunlight played over his brown body. "The starting of the journey depends upon Soul. For Soul alone must consciously make Its attempt to put the feet there. The Sat Guru is always waiting, and he never in any way attempts to persuade the disciple to make the step."

The seeker swam through the clean, sparkling brown water, then pulled himself upon the sandy bank and stretched out. His body was vibrating with a million shooting electrical sparks.

"What is the purpose of the divine journey?" he asked softly, looking at the wonderful physique of the Traveler stretched out on the sandy shore. "Where does man go and how does he travel over the path to God?"

"The misunderstanding lies within the mind roots," replied Rebazar Tarzs, raising himself and staring at a small water snake that swam gracefully through the water and up to the shore. It wiggled up to the Traveler's feet and coiled up close to them. Reaching down he stroked its tiny head with a gentle hand. "You see this little creature which always creates fear in man? It is on the divine journey to God's Home, yet it knows not that. It responds to the divine love which is being given it, and will not bite until I arouse the opposite.

179

"The divine journey begins in the highest creation of God; or, in other words, it starts with the unconscious masses of spiritual atoms and angels which lie at God's feet in the true eternal Home.

"In order to have a harmonious place in the highest world, God sends all these into His kingdoms, even to the lowest, in order to become experienced in all the spiritual experiences which are possible. Therefore, you, as the perfected atom within, are not of the greatest value to God until you have become truly realized within of thy own divinity.

"You must first know thyself, and then know God. And this is truth from every plane in ITS whole creation.

"So you start from Heaven when God sends each Soul into the world of the material planes, and you light upon this earth in the tiniest form as an amoeba, and then the journey to return to thine own true Home starts.

"You will work thy own way through the millions of myriad forms which God has manifested upon this earth, upward into man, and then thy real suffering begins, for the Real Self knows that It must reach the apex of all God's creations, including the angels and archangels which surround God's own throne. Yet man does not recognize himself, and the struggle upon the Wheel of the Eighty-Four really starts.

"Reincarnation is established within the life of man, and he struggles through the mire and the morass which surround him. His mind is blinded by its own clouds of illusion for greatness, and he believes that all begins in the mind and ends in the mind. That nothing is greater than the mind. It is nothing unusual, for the mind creates false values and establishes itself as the greatness of man.

"And let me tell you, my young friend, that the mind has great power and it creates such illusions that man thinks that this is God and worships it as God. The mind power creates a false body known to you as ego, or false self, and man knowing this self thinks of it as Soul.

"This false self has great pride in its own doings and it works for its own existence and fights the true Self that is ambitious for only one ideal—to return to God forever, to get through with Its experiences in this world and go home again.

"Then the desire of Soul becomes so great that somewhere and sometime the ECK Guru appears and finds the perfected being hidden behind the false self, and knowing this, he establishes the feet of that Soul upon Its true path, or the divine journey homeward.

"The Master gives only three requirements for the devotee; they are to have purity of Soul, to have the true teacher, and to follow the instructions of the true teacher who gives you the secrets of the Light and Sound.

"The Light is to illuminate the path for the devotee, and the Sound is that which Soul follows back to Its true source, like the lamb follows the shepherd's flute. This only is the secret, and there are no others. Until you see and look, nothing will be clear for thine own eyes, and you will not be able to make progress upon thy own divine journey!"

The little snake hissed and slithered closer to the teacher's foot, and settled down under the stroking of its tiny head. Rebazar smiled and raised his gaze to the seeker, who felt the power of God suddenly flowing through him.

Jewels of Wisdom

ell me about wisdom, O Sire," said the seeker as the two walked through the fields on the island which bridged the two rivers. "I desire to know of wisdom." The Tibetan plucked a blade of grass and chewed its fresh sweetness.

"Get thee first understanding, my son," said the Traveler, "and then you shall have wisdom. To have understanding you must have total awareness of the inner self at all times."

"Then how do I have total awareness, Sire?" asked the seeker.

"By fixing thy mind on God!" replied the Tibetan without concern.

The seeker's gaze wandered, touching upon the distant peaks, saw the sun in the midheavens and the glory of its light upon the river. Across the waters of the river on their left sat the little city like a mother watching its children, unconcerned about all, yet watchful that none go out of her sight.

He said, "How does one fix his mind on God?"

"By repeating the sacred name of the Lord," said Rebazar, "and singing ITS glories, and visiting God's devotees and holy men. The mind cannot dwell on God if it is immersed day and night in worldliness, in worldly duties and responsibilities; it is most necessary

185

to go into solitude now and then and think of God. To fix the mind on God is difficult in the beginning, unless one practices the Spiritual Exercises of ECK in solitude.

"I tell you this. There are three exercises one practices: think of God while doing thine own duties, or contemplate God in a secluded corner of thine own house, or contemplate IT in a woods. And you should always discriminate between the real and the unreal. God alone is real, the eternal substance; all else is unreal, that is, impermanent. By discriminating thus one should shut out the impermanent objects from the mind.

"To live in this world you must do all thy duties, but keep thy mind on God. Live with all, thy own beloved and thy family, and serve them. Treat them with great reverence, and great love, but know that they do not belong to thee. So do as I say—do all thy own duties in this world, but keep thy mind on God.

"If you try to live in this world without cultivating love for God, you will be entangled more and more. You will be overwhelmed with its dangers, its griefs, and its sorrows. And the more you think of worldly things, the more you will be in need of them. Secure the oil of divine love, and then put thyself to the task of thine own duties of this world.

"So I tell you that by being with God in solitude the mind acquires knowledge and devotion. But the very same mind goes downward if it is disturbed by the very waves of those who seek to disturb you in thy search for God.

"It is always possible to see God. But you must do as I say; repeat the sacred names, and do all thy work in ITS name, for ITS sake, and without expectations of reward. Then you will see God in all ITS glory.

"Above all, you must have faith in thy own power to reach God, and then have faith in thy Guru who is the Godman, and who can show you God; and then have faith in the supreme being which comes to you because you have faith in all. Faith is one of the essentials of the path to reach and dwell in God.

"God is beyond vidya and avidya, knowledge and ignorance. He is beyond all maya, the illusion of duality.

"One attains the knowledge of God in the ECK and at the same time one realizes God. It is in this state that man, the seeker, stops all reasoning and his tongue is silent. He has no power to describe the nature of God.

"When man has dwelled in God through inner silence for any length of time, he must return to the earth again. He finds that it is God who has now become the earth and its living beings. He even finds that God has become the false self within himself, and all other creation; that he of himself cannot even create the false without the help of God.

"The path of wisdom leads to Truth, as does the path that combines knowledge and love. The path of love, too, leads to this goal. The way of love is better than wisdom and understanding, for with love you can have all. All paths ultimately lead to God, so do not fret if another person is not willing to see God as you see Him, nor look upon your Sat Guru as you look upon him, nor look upon this world as you look upon it.

"All are traveling the path to God."

The Tibetan motioned toward the boat pulled upon the shore of the island. They got into it, and the seeker took the oars and started pulling downstream toward their rendezvous.

The Riddle of God

he seeker and his teacher stood at the edge of the river, near the old oak tree, looking out over the brown, muddy water which flowed onward toward the sea. The sun was rising over the hills, casting long lances of light across the forest, shores, and rivers.

Tears glistened in the eyes of the seeker as he turned to the Master. "I want to stay with thee forever, O Sire," he pleaded. "Must I go again? I am wearied and tired and need thy comfort."

"I am always with you, unto the end of the world," said Rebazar Tarzs gently, with one hand on the seeker's shoulder. "You have thine own work to do in this world with thy beloved at thy side. Ye must go and do."

He spoke again, "Ye are to carry the word of God into this world, unceasingly and without hesitation. Never be concerned, for I am always with thee, guiding thee and helping thee in every way. My heart goes with thee.

"I tell ye that ye must be as Jesus told his disciples, 'Be ye therefore wise as serpents, and harmless as doves.' Harm nothing, but always keep in thy own heart the very love of God for all ITS creations, and then no harm can come to thee. Revere thy own fellow beings and all creatures of the heart. Look to God for wisdom, understanding, and guidance. IT will give thee all when thy heart is tired and sore and weary.

"There is no burden that is too great for God. Take whatever IT gives with the fullest grace of thy heart, and never feel that ye are without IT. God's grace and mercy will pour upon ye, every moment of the day and night. IT will watch over thee like the shepherd watches over his flock at all hours.

"My instruction with thee is finished at the present, and only in Spirit will I give thee guidance while ye are in this world.

"I have only one last thing to tell thee. This is it, and it must be impressed forever upon thy mind, until we meet again; and be not alarmed for we shall meet again within a year from this time, upon the very spot where we now stand.

"I wish to declare the riddle of God to thee. It is most important that this be done. Listen closely and understand. The riddle of God is this.

"God is what ye believe IT is. No man is wrong about the existence of God, and yet no man is right about his knowledge of God. There is no mystery in God except that IT is what each Soul believes that IT is.

So the riddle is that; but all men will quarrel and argue about the greatness of God and their own knowledge of Him.

"Yet every man is right in his knowledge of God. But does this mean that the drunkard is as right as the great minister who preaches from the pulpit? Yea, I say that he, the drunkard, is as much upon the path as the preacher is in his pulpit. Ah, but this is justified in thy thinking. Each is in his own place according to his understanding. Ah, but there is the answer.

"If the drunkard seeks God through his bottle, and it seems irreverent to speak of both in the same breath, then let it be. But I mean to tell ye that the seeking of happiness, be it on a material plane or spiritual plane, is the seeking of God. The ideal of the drunkard is to become drunk and unconscious so he can forget all and dwell within himself in a state of happiness. The God-seeker wishes to become unconscious in a state of inner silence to forget all and dwell in a state of happiness within. What is the difference?

"None, I tell ye, for the drunkard may be closer to God than the God-seeker who with all his intensity for the SUGMAD may drive IT away. On the other hand, the drunkard will in his drunkenness forget himself, his selfishness, and false self, and it being this way, may have God's mercy granted him and lo, the enlightenment comes.

"Only two things pervade upon the seeker or the drunkard. Both must be interested in what they seek, be it God or selfish interest. Both must have concentrated upon what they are seeking, and in finding it must believe in it.

"The only difference is usually purity of character and ideals. But who knows what thy fellowman has in his heart unless his tongue or deeds reveal such? And such is the riddle of God. God will come to anyone who needs Him, regardless of what their state of character or ideals may be.

"This is the riddle of God!

"Now farewell, and hurry home!" said the Tibetan embracing the seeker in his great arms. "I will expect to see ye again when the April blossoms fill the air by the river Jhelum again!"

The seeker turned away and walked off into the distance, as Rebazar watched until he disappeared over a hillock. Then the Tibetan took up a handful of rice and threw it into the water. As the fish nibbled on it he looked down and spoke.

"So be the way of God, little brothers, so be the way of God. All is well in His world with thyselves, thy brothers, and me!"

BARAKA BASHAD.

May the Blessings Be.

Glossary

Words set in SMALL CAPS are defined elsewhere in the glossary.

ARAHATA. An experienced and qualified teacher for ECKANKAR classes.

CHELA. A spiritual student.

ECK. The Life Force, the Holy Spirit, or Audible Life Current which sustains all life.

ECKANKAR. Religion of the Light and Sound of God. Also known as the Ancient Science of SOUL TRAVEL. A truly spiritual religion for the individual in modern times, known as the secret path to God via dreams and SOUL TRAVEL. The teachings provide a framework for anyone to explore their own spiritual experiences. Established by Paul Twitchell, the modern-day founder, in 1965.

ECK MASTERS. Spiritual Masters who can assist and protect people in their spiritual studies and travels. The ECK Masters are from a long line of God-Realized SOULS who know the responsibility that goes with spiritual freedom.

HU. The secret name for God. The singing of the word HU, pronounced like the word *hue*, is considered a love song to God. It is sung in the ECK Worship Service.

INITIATION. Earned by the ECK member through spiritual unfoldment and service to God. The initiation is a private ceremony in which the individual is linked to the Sound and Light of God.

LIVING ECK MASTER. The title of the spiritual leader of ECKANKAR. His duty is to lead SOULS back to God. The Living ECK Master can assist spiritual students physically as the Outer Master, in the dream state as the Dream Master, and in the spiritual worlds as the Inner Master. Sri Harold Klemp became the Living ECK Master in 1981.

MAHANTA. A title to describe the highest state of God Consciousness on earth, often embodied in the LIVING ECK MASTER. He is the Living Word.

PLANES. The levels of heaven, such as the Astral, Causal, Mental, Etheric, and Soul planes.

SATSANG. A class in which students of ECK study a monthly lesson from ECKANKAR.

THE SHARIYAT-KI-SUGMAD. The sacred scriptures of ECKANKAR. The scriptures are comprised of twelve volumes in the spiritual worlds. The first two were transcribed from the inner PLANES by Paul Twitchell, modern-day founder of ECKANKAR.

SOUL. The True Self. The inner, most sacred part of each person. Soul exists before birth and lives on after the death of the physical body. As a spark of God, Soul can see, know, and perceive all things. It is the creative center of Its own world.

SOUL TRAVEL. The expansion of consciousness. The ability of SOUL to transcend the physical body and travel into the spiritual worlds of God. Soul Travel is taught only by the LIVING ECK MASTER. It helps people unfold spiritually and can provide proof of the existence of God and life after death.

SOUND AND LIGHT OF ECK. The Holy Spirit. The two aspects through which God appears in the lower worlds. People can experience them by looking and listening within themselves and through SOUL TRAVEL.

SPIRITUAL EXERCISES OF ECK. The daily practice of certain techniques to get us in touch with the Light and Sound of God.

SUGMAD. A sacred name for God. SUGMAD is neither masculine nor feminine; IT is the source of all life.

WAH Z. The spiritual name of Sri Harold Klemp. It means the Secret Doctrine. It is his name in the spiritual worlds.

How to Learn More about ECKANKAR
Religion of the Light and Sound of God

Why are you as important to God as any famous head of state, priest, minister, or saint that ever lived?

- Do you know God's purpose in your life?
- Why does God's Will seem so unpredictable?
- Why do you talk to God, but practice no one religion?

ECKANKAR can show you why special attention from God is neither random nor reserved for the few known saints. But it is for every individual. It is for anyone who opens himself to Divine Spirit, the Light and Sound of God.

People want to know the secrets of life and death. In response to this need Sri Harold Klemp, today's spiritual leader of ECKANKAR, and Paul Twitchell, its modern-day founder, have written a series of monthly discourses that give specialized Spiritual Exercises of ECK. They can lead Soul in a direct way to God.

Those who wish to study ECKANKAR can receive these special monthly discourses which give clear, simple instructions for these spiritual exercises.

Membership in ECKANKAR Includes

1. The opportunity to gain wisdom, charity, and spiritual freedom.
2. Twelve monthly discourses which include information on Soul, the spiritual meaning of dreams, Soul Travel techniques, and ways to establish a personal relationship with Divine Spirit. You may study them alone at home or in a class with others.
3. The *Mystic World,* a quarterly newsletter with a Wisdom Note and articles by the Living ECK Master. In it are also letters and articles from members of ECKANKAR around the world.
4. Special mailings to keep you informed of upcoming ECKANKAR seminars and activities worldwide, new study materials available from ECKANKAR, and more.
5. The opportunity to attend ECK Satsang classes and book discussions with others in your community.
6. Initiation eligibility.
7. Attendance at certain meetings for members of ECKANKAR at ECK seminars.

How to Find Out More

To request membership in ECKANKAR using your credit card (or for a free booklet on membership) call (612) 544-0066, weekdays, between 8:00 a.m. and 5:00 p.m., central time. Or write to: ECKANKAR, Att: Information, P.O. Box 27300, Minneapolis, MN 55427 U.S.A.

Introductory Books on ECKANKAR

Cloak of Consciousness,
Mahanta Transcripts, Book 5
Harold Klemp

Often we insulate ourselves from the harsh world of pressures, fears, and problems. You can replace this cocoon of fears with the mantle of God's love, the cloak of consciousness. Harold Klemp, the spiritual leader of ECKANKAR, can help you drop long-held fears. He shows you how to experience the Light and Sound of God through the Spiritual Exercises of ECKANKAR and find spiritual freedom.

Ask the Master, Book 1
Harold Klemp

Do you find yourself asking, What is my purpose in life? Are dreams real? How do past lives affect us today? Harold Klemp, as the spiritual leader of ECKANKAR, clearly and candidly answers many questions which have plagued mankind throughout history. He also addresses questions contained in thousands of letters he receives from around the globe. His answers can help you overcome fear; learn self-discipline; be more creative; and improve family relationships.

ECKANKAR—Ancient Wisdom for Today

Are you one of the millions who have heard God speak to you through a profound spiritual experience? This introductory book will show you how dreams, Soul Travel, and experiences with past lives are ways God speaks to you. An enjoyable, easy-to-read approach to ECKANKAR. After reading this little book, you'll emerge with new perspectives on your spiritual life.

The Wind of Change
Harold Klemp

What are the hidden spiritual reasons behind every event in your life? With stories drawn from his own lifelong training, ECKANKAR's spiritual leader shows you how to use the power of Divine Spirit to discover those reasons. Follow him from the Wisconsin farm of his youth to a military base in Japan; from a job in Texas into the realms beyond, as he shares the secrets of ECKANKAR.

For fastest service, phone (612) 544-0066 weekdays between 8:00 a.m. and 5:00 p.m., central time, to request books using your credit card, or look under **ECKANKAR** in your phone book for an ECKANKAR Center near you. Or write: **ECKANKAR, Att: Information, P.O. Box 27300, Minneapolis, MN 55427 U.S.A.**

There May Be an
ECKANKAR Study Group near You

ECKANKAR offers a variety of local and international activities for the spiritual seeker. With hundreds of study groups worldwide, ECKANKAR is near you! Many areas have ECKANKAR Centers where you can browse through the books in a quiet, unpressured environment, talk with others who share an interest in this ancient teaching, and attend beginning discussion classes on how to gain the attributes of Soul: wisdom, power, love, and freedom.

Around the world, ECKANKAR study groups offer special one-day or weekend seminars on the basic teachings of ECKANKAR. Check your phone book under **ECKANKAR**, or call **(612) 544-0066** for membership information and the location of the ECKANKAR Center or study group nearest you. Or write **ECKANKAR, Att: Information, P.O. Box 27300, Minneapolis, MN 55427 U.S.A.**

☐ Please send me information on the nearest ECKANKAR discussion or study group in my area.

☐ Please send me more information about membership in ECKANKAR, which includes a twelve-month spiritual study.

Please type or print clearly   940

Name _____

Street_____ Apt. # _____

City _____ State/Prov. _____

ZIP/Postal Code _____ Country _____